ONCE THERE WERE
GIANTS

Other Books by Jerry Izenberg

Non-Fiction

Rozelle: A Biography

Through My Eyes: A Sports Writer's 58-Year Journey

No Medals for Trying: A Week in the Life of a Pro Football Team

The Jerry Izenberg Collection

How Many Miles to Camelot?: The All-American Sport Myth

New York Giants: Seventy-Five Years

The Greatest Game Ever Played

Great Latin Sports Figures: The Proud People

The Rivals

At Large With Jerry Izenberg

Championship: The NFL Title Games Plus Super Bowl

Novels

After the Fire: Land Hate in the Ashes of 1967

ONCE THERE WERE GIANTS

THE GOLDEN AGE OF HEAVYWEIGHT BOXING

Jerry Izenberg

Foreword by Manny Pacquiao

Skyhorse Publishing

A Herman Graf Book

In memory of Ray and Stephanie Arcel,
who touched my family with both love and knowledge

Photo credit: Arlene Schulman

Contents

Once upon a time, of all the magic moments in ballparks and arenas from California to New York, there was nothing to rival that magic moment that could grab a heavyweight fight crowd by its collective jugular vein and trigger a tsunami of raw emotion from it before a single punch had been thrown.

That's the way it was when there were heavyweight giants . . . when no ersatz drama had to be generated by high roller hotels for the fighters' entries into the ring . . . no smoke, mirrors, and noise trying to disguise itself as music. Instead, these were crowds that truly knew what had brought them to this moment—it was the fighters, the ones who eclipsed other newsmakers in every newspaper sports section. Back then, in all of sports, nothing dominated the public eye like a heavyweight championship fight.

It's not the same today. I am reminded of a single recent moment that illustrates the fact that the heavyweight division has since lost its way from old tunes of glory and has degenerated into a carnival sideshow.

The lights in what used to be known as Atlantic City's Convention Hall had dimmed. Music that can best be described as a hymn to the tone-deaf fills the air. A fight manager named Lou Duva is trying to shove his fighter out of the tunnel and into the arena.

"Goddammit, get out there," he screams.

"I ain't budgin' until I hear my music. That ain't my music. I want my music or I don't go."

"Yeah," Duva almost spits the words in his face. "I'm sure Joe Louis would have said the same thing, you dumb shit."

So, where are America's heavyweight giants today? Gone like the dodo bird or the Edsel or the sundial—and they ain't never coming back. Look for them, instead, playing tight end or linebacker in the National Football League or power forward in the NBA, positions with job descriptions that do not demand the brutal directness of a left uppercut to the chin or a ferocious right hand to the solar plexus.

In most cases, you will find what's left of the fading heavyweights in Eastern Europe, living on a diet of potatoes and more potatoes. Hunger and pride makes heavyweight giants. Suffice it to say that you will not see any Harvard PhD candidates spurning hedge fund offers for 6 a.m. roadwork and a spot on the undercard in Stockton, California.

The obvious truth here is that there will never again be a heavyweight cycle like the one that began when Sonny Liston stopped Floyd Patterson—and ended when Mike Tyson bit a slice out of Evander Holyfield's ear.

This is about a precious loss in both the history and sociology of America that has earned the right to be remembered.

Once there were giants . . . and I was there to witness it.

FOREWORD
BY MANNY PACQUIAO

This is about the real history of heavyweight boxing. Of course, it includes Muhammad Ali. That part is obvious, but you may be surprised to learn that that in this book the operative words beyond the great fighters include Prohibition, gangsters and much more.

Jerry Izenberg, a giant of a writer, has dominated his field. His prose carries the power of a George Foreman right cross; His descriptions seamlessly conjure up a panorama of the heavyweight scene from champion to champion with the perfection of Ali's footwork. I'm not surprised. Izenberg has been doing it for seven decades.

Once There Were Giants: The Golden Age of Heavyweight Boxing is a journey through a time that reveals the good, the bad and the ugly of a brutal but beautiful sport that most fans see only in terms of knockouts.

Izenberg's vivid description takes you to a New York City of the Prohibition Era and the business model of a speakeasy owner named Ownie Madden. Madden was an entrepreneur, a thug and a murderer. With those talents he turned heavyweight boxing into his private fiefdom.

Ultimately, he was replaced by men even more ruthless. The last of that group were named Frankie Carbo who rose through Mafia

ranks from strong man to assassin and his henchman, Blinky Palermo. Izenberg knew them and now so do we. In this book he writes
of the men they killed, the fighters they owned and the power both
lost.

Because he is a brilliant storyteller this is more than a boxing
book. It is American history…. a nation divided before the first Ali-
Frazier fight--and Jerry was there…the night in Las Vegas that Mike
Tyson chewed off a hunk of Evander Holyfield's ear—and Jerry was
there to tell you what Holyfield said to the referee and why he insisted the fight continue…15 rounds of hell between Larry Holmes
and Ken Norton, perhaps the greatest single heavyweight round of
all—and Jerry was there.

He knew them, Ali, Liston. Holmes, the Spinks Brothers—all
of them. Most of all he is a brilliant storyteller, what was Ali's Deer
Lake training camp really like? …the tragedy of Ron Lyle…the desperate quest for redemption by George Foreman…was there a real or
a phantom punch in Ali-Liston II? …why Joe Frazier and Muhammad Ali never really buried their feud.

Jerry Izenberg has seen boxing's best and worst of times. He
weaves them together in a fascinating tapestry in this book. The excitement he generates jumps out at you like Joe Frazier's left hook.

It's almost enough to make me wish I was a heavyweight.

Manny "Pacman" Pacquiao,
the only man in history to win championships
in eight different weight classes

PROLOGUE

The Accidental Fight Fan

Newark, New Jersey, 1938

I was eight years old, three years younger than my sister and very much a part of our baseball-addicted family, which figured because my dad in his youth had been a minor league second baseman, living out a dream that in the end—like those of so many other young men of his time—came up short. Long before I was born, he was already working long, tough hours in the dye house that would eventually kill him. One day, during one of those private moments fathers and sons often don't have enough of, he told me that in the past there were times when he was the only Jew in his league, let alone on his team. He was no stranger to anti-Semitism.

Thinking back, some of my fondest memories are of those soft summer nights when my father, my sister, and I would listen on our old Philco to the feeble attempts of Carl Hubbell and Mel Ott trying to make National League contenders out of the New York Giants. But then along came Hank Greenberg, the home run hitter from the playing fields of New York City who had been totally ignored by the Giants and Yankees. He was a Detroit Tiger, but he became "the man" in our house. The Giants could wait. My father had found a Jewish superstar.

Our supper table belonged to Hank. It was the summer that this kid from Erasmus High School took off in hot pursuit of Babe Ruth's single-season home run record of 60. However, he would be stopped at 58 home runs, two short of Ruth's record. But this was America of the 1930s. Ruth was an icon, and the national mood then did not look favorably on a Jewish hero replacing a baseball legend. Neither did the players. Some pitchers intentionally walked him so he couldn't swing the bat. They threw at his head. My dad took this all very personally.

With his interest in Greenberg, I can never remember the supper table conversation turning to football or basketball, or what my dad considered the alien games of ice hockey and soccer. And most of all, I don't remember a single discussion of boxing.

Of course, before my time, my dad had been an intense follower of the fortunes of the great Jewish lightweight champion, Benny Leonard. It was Benny who Americanized the immigrants of New York's Lower East Side. In their fractured English, they lovingly referred to Leonard as "The Great Bennah."

That was all I ever heard him say about boxing, until June 22, 1938.

Unaware of it at the time, I was the one who set it in motion. I had been walking home from a neighbor's house earlier that week and was attracted by a chalk-scrawl on the sidewalk.

It read: "All Jews Are Kites."

I was only eight years old, but there were some things I knew as gospel. One of them was the fact that I was Jewish; the other was that I was reasonably sure I couldn't fly. When I asked my father what it meant that night, he told me, "First, it means that it was written by an illiterate moron, which most anti-Semites are. Second, the word is *kike*. Put up your fists. No, not like that, heaven help us—higher, closer to your chin. Good. Now listen carefully. If anyone—and I mean anyone—calls you that to your face, I want you to smile at him so he relaxes, and then hit him in the mouth with a right hand, and if you don't finish with the left hook I taught you, don't bother coming home."

I do not believe he meant that last part, but I know he meant the first.

This, obviously, was a precursor to what happened at the supper table later in the week.

"Tonight," my father said, "I don't want to hear about any of those radio shows you like. Tonight we are all going to listen to the Louis–Schmeling fight. This colored man [not unusual terminology in 1938] is fighting for us as Americans, for us as Jews, and for all the colored people in America." There followed a lecture on Hitler, the Nazis, and the Jews, and what he feared was about to happen in Europe and who knew where else.

The very morning of the fight, fifteen German-Americans were actually arrested as spies for Nazi Germany. There was no doubt that night, as we gathered in the living room where the radio was, that the fists of Joe Louis would be the fists of David, who in earlier times went against Goliath with just five smooth stones. They would attack the man who represented Adolf Hitler. Decades later, I would get to know both men well. I would learn that Max Schmeling was not a Nazi and that Joe Louis's ferocity during that fight had nothing to do with anything except for the fact that Schmeling had knocked him out two years earlier.

But 1938 was the time of the resurgence of the Klan and the German-American Bund; the anti-Semitic radio broadcast obscenities of Father Coughlin, the radio priest of Royal Oak, Michigan, who hid behind his collar and his microphone; and, closer to home in New Jersey, the anti-Catholic, anti-black, and anti-Jewish babbling of a buffoon named Conde McGinley and his obscene newspaper, *Common Sense*.

At supper that night, nobody mentioned Hank Greenberg. Even my mother sat along with us and waited for a fight that we had reason to believe was representative of "us" against "them."

Half a century later, in a tiny all-black town in Jefferson Parish, Louisiana, a man named Calvin Wilkerson told me he had experienced the same feeling that day in 1938, although we both didn't know it at the time.

"I can guess just how your daddy felt," the elderly black man told me, "because that's the way it was for us each time Joe fought. It wasn't just Joe in the ring—it was us, too. Three months after the fight, a young black man named R. C. Williams was castrated and lynched six miles up the road in Ruston and left hanging from a tree for five days."

This was the story of how I found a hero and came to boxing by accident. It was the night my dad and Calvin Wilkerson, who never knew each other, became brothers under the skin as they yelled themselves hoarse the instant Louis drove Schmeling into the ropes a heartbeat after the opening bell.

I remember jumping up along with them to yell pretty much the same things, as Louis rained combinations down on Schmeling, who was badly shaken. He froze him there and finished it with his trademark left hook, the one to the solar plexus—quicker than a cobra and twice as deadly, one so short and so quick that even sports writers rarely saw it, one that traveled just six inches but made the following right hand that everyone saw merely window dressing. Schmeling never had a chance. And in the hearts of Jerry Izenberg and Calvin Wilkerson, and the thousands along the way of every color and ethnicity with whom I shared that golden memory, the soft-spoken Joe Louis lives in the backroads of our minds with a gentle ferocity that battered down walls higher and meaner than those of Jericho.

Decades after Joe's salad years, when he desperately needed money, a fight promoter paid him to publicly support an inept contender's title chances. As he leaned against the ring ropes during that workout, I remember hollering, "Joe, move to your left. You're blocking my view." "You don't know how lucky you are," he replied. "You don't know how lucky you are."

Clearly, for all his problems, Joe Louis never lost his timing.

There is a bond between fighters that outsiders never get to understand. When Sonny Liston died, on the night before his funeral, a man named Abe Margolis told Louis, "Frank (Sinatra) and Sammy (Davis) will be here tonight. We are all going to the funeral together, Joe, so be here at 9 a.m. sharp. No excuses." Margolis was the man who founded the highly successful Zale's jewelry chain. In New York, he was respected by celebrities, with boxes at Yankee Stadium, the Polo Grounds, and Ebbets Field, as well as ringside at Madison Square Garden, and fifth row center at Broadway openings.

Joe Louis was special to Margolis. Louis had become a greeter at Caesars Palace, where Margolis was a high roller. Each time he came to Vegas, he was sure to slip two hundred-dollar bills into Louis's sports jacket pocket. When Margolis spoke, Louis listened.

But the next morning at 9 a.m. sharp, there was no Louis. Ten minutes later, Margolis told his group, "We can't leave. I know where to look."

He found Louis at a crap table with bets all over the board.

"Joe, we're late."

"Abe, I just made six passes."

"Joe, we're late."

Louis held up the dice, blew on them, raised them toward the ceiling, and smiled and said, "Abe, Sonny would understand."

And I think he would have.

Just as surely as that left hook of his traveled only six inches, Louis always used an economy of words to make his point. He was the greatest heavyweight I—and I believe anyone else—ever saw. But you won't read about him again in this book about the golden era of heavyweights . . . not him, not Rocky Marciano, not Jack Johnson. Their greatness is not diminished, because the truth is they did not have many guys good enough to fight them in their eras.

But those who follow next were the giants who fought other giants; giants who never ducked anyone in a waiting army of authentic contenders. They were the champions and challengers who made the years from 1962 through 1997 a genuine heavyweight boxing Val-halla. This book is about that magical time, and the best of the best, the likes of which we shall never see again.

It also must be said that during this era, a multiplicity of self-styled boxing governing bodies who were so inept, highly bribable, or just plain stupid, did indeed also bestow ersatz titles on transient and tissue-paper heavyweights.

You won't read about those ships in the night here. At least four fighters who came afterward might have been in that company: the Klitschko Brothers, Lennox Lewis, and Riddick Bowe. But like Louis, Marciano, and Johnson, they did have an army of worthy op-ponents. They are at least noted in this book, if only barely.

Once upon a time, you could have asked almost anybody on the street who the current heavyweight champion was, and he would have told you. Ultimately, boxing reached a point when no one had an answer, because the truth was nobody believed a champion existed anymore, except for those the alphabet soup of boxing organizations had designated. I have been at thousands of ringsides on my journey as a newspaperman. It's why I know exactly who belongs here. This is about the real ones of that glorious time when everybody fought each other . . . a time when the genuine champions stood out like the Hope Diamond, measured against a field of broken soda bottles.

Trust me on this. If Joe Louis were here, he would understand this just as clearly as he believed Sonny Liston would have under-stood him that morning when he stood at the crap table in Las Vegas with a hot hand, waving the dice toward Heaven.

Henderson, Nevada, 2015

ONE

Tough Guys Have Rules

A friend of mine, Rodger Donahue, a ranked middleweight in the 1950s with a ferocious left hook, used to delight in telling the story of the night Frank Costello, the Murder, Inc. mobster, took his girlfriend to the old Stork Club and invited three world champions to join them. This must have been on a Friday night, because New York mobsters always reserved Saturday night for their wives.

Once they were all seated, Costello demanded each of them dance with his lady. In those days, a request from Costello was tantamount to a request you couldn't refuse.

But the boxer Willie Pep refused. And the mobster wasn't offended, because Pep retorted with an argument Costello couldn't refute: "Tough guys don't dance."

Because it said so much about ersatz machismo, Norman Mailer took it for the title of one of his novels. And in understanding the once verdant relationship between mobsters and boxers, Costello's acceptance of that phrase is more than a notion. It is a road map into the thinking of the obsession that the family of tightly-knit mobsters has always had with the whole business of boxing.

It is why, on that night, Costello, the *capo di tutti capi* of the Genovese crime family, tolerated what other practitioners of raw power and hired muscle might have considered a direct insult—and he took it from featherweight Willie Pep, who weighed 126 pounds. If Pep, a world champion, said that's what tough guys didn't do, then Costello, who like most mobsters prized his own toughness, understood.

This was how it generally was with those members of the mob who muscled their way in until they controlled most of boxing— that is, until the night Muhammad Ali left the last mob-controlled fighter, Sonny Liston, slumped over on his own stool in abject defeat.

It is probably true that the mob had no influence on the out-come of the famous Cain–Abel fight. After all, even they knew an authority much higher than the Eden Boxing Commission had han-dled that decision. But we can say that here, in the United States, it was common knowledge that the mob was fixing fights as far back as the start of the twentieth century.

The first boxing godfather arrived in New York City in 1901. He was Liverpool-born Owen "Owney" Vincent Madden, who immi-grated here as a teenager with his mother. Their first home was a tenement in Manhattan's Hell's Kitchen, an area of roughly twenty-five blocks between the Hudson River and Eighth Avenue. It was poor, overcrowded, and in the main predominantly populated by Irish and English immigrants. Owney Madden was a ferocious street fighter, but boxing wasn't on his mind. What was, was escape. The poverty of Hell's Kitchen bred more than its share of violence. Much of midtown Manhattan back then was a city of gangs, including the Gophers, whom Madden led as a kind of war counselor, which continually battled the rival Dusters for neighborhood supremacy.

He established the supremacy of his gang, along with his own role as king of the avenue. In record time, Madden was alleged to have killed five of the rival gang members over an extended period.

In 1912, he killed another one over a woman's affections. By then, he had acquired the nickname "the Killer." In one of the toughest neighborhoods in a city on the make, Owney Madden was the ultimate player.

Not surprisingly, while the gang wars gave him a fear-tinged aura of respect, they also sharpened another skill that would threaten to destroy him—treachery. Cloaked in the guise of bringing peace to Hell's Kitchen, Madden offered to meet a rival gang leader named Doyle to talk about a definitive truce. He was so publicly committed to it that he went to the meeting well ahead of schedule. That timing enabled him to shoot Doyle in the head on November 28, 1914, from ambush, thereby leaving his rival just a little bit dead. Until then, he had never been convicted of anything because his evil charisma had always enabled him to cast a spell that seemed to render all witnesses deaf, mute, and blind. This time, the magic went out of Madden's smile, and the terror leaked out of his threats. The neighborhood sang like an *a cappella* chorus of canaries. He was sentenced to twenty years in Sing Sing, served only nine, and came out looking for work.

He found it as a strong arm man for a major bootlegger while he freelanced his own bootlegging gig, founded a profitable "join-or-else" cab driver union, and blossomed among the speakeasies as a man about town. He wound up owning the Cotton Club of Harlem Renaissance fame, where most of the customers were white and all of the performing artists were black.

During this period, he hired his own full-time chauffeur as befits a man with deep pockets and a gigantic ego. The driver was named George Raft, which may explain why Raft later won Hollywood acclaim for his gangster roles in films. Raft had had the perfect teacher.

Madden earned his bones as a bootlegger and saloon keeper of some prominence. He had already earned them as a killer. His favorite Manhattan night spot was a speakeasy known as Billy LaHiff's, a regular hangout for athletes, show business people, socialites, and thugs. By then, in 1931, he had already joined forces with two boxing musclemen, "Broadway" Bill Duffy and George Jean "Big Frenchie" DeMange. Madden was clearly the boss and controlled a number of prominent fighters, including the heavyweight-champ-in-waiting, Max Baer.

What followed was an event that stamped Madden as a mobster who, for a time, was one of the first underworld kings of boxing. The story was told to me in detail by the late Willie "The Beard" Gilzenberg, so-called because his beard was so heavy he shaved twice a day. Gilzenberg ruled boxing in Newark, New Jersey, where he promoted from two fight clubs: a minor league ballpark and the National Guard Armory. This story about Madden was so blatant, and so off the wall, that you couldn't make it up if you tried. Gilzenberg didn't have to try. He had been there.

At that time, Madden was a man in motion. Between his businesses (both legal and illegal), he strode Broadway like a colossus, generally in the company of Duffy and other members of his gang. Shadowing Madden virtually every night was a Broadway character named Walter "Good Time Charley" Friedman.

Friedman was a dreamer and a con man, not necessarily in that order. From Stillman's Gym to Jack and Charlie's 21 Club speakeasy, and up and down Broadway, he tried to sell an opportunistic story of a heavyweight title as yet unborn. Madden, who was the most powerful mark he could find, was his main target.

"Listen," Friedman kept saying. "Like I been telling you, there is a tribe of giants over in China. All we got to do is get the biggest, strongest giant they got, bring him back, and we got the heavyweight champeen of the world."

Madden had heard that pitch a thousand times. One night in LaHiff's, at a table with his colleagues and Gilzenberg, he silently debated whether to break both of Friedman's arms or finally throw him a bone. Finally, as the others rocked the room with their raucous laughter, Madden threw five hundred dollars on the table and said, "Get the hell outta here. Go to fuckin' China and don't show your ugly face to me again until you bring me the giant."

And so Friedman disappeared from the Broadway after-dark scene.

Six months later, a cable from London was delivered to LaHiff's after midnight. It was no mystery how Friedman found Madden; he knew that no evening for Madden could possibly end without a slice of LaHiff's cheesecake. The usual suspects were gathered there. The cable read: "Have found the giant. Will arrive in New York City next week."

How did Friedman confuse London for China? Clearly he missed a lot of geography classes. But it is here that two new critical characters enter this narrative: the promoter Frenchman Léon See and Primo Carnera.

Carnera was 6 feet, 6 inches tall and 218 pounds—the biggest man in boxing for more than a decade—so big that the New York Athletic Commission (nicknamed colloquially "the Three Dumb Dukes") tried to create a new boxing weight division, the dreadnought class. It dictated it would approve no fighter as a Carnera opponent weighing fewer than around 200 pounds. As a point of reference, the great Jack Dempsey, the heavyweight champion a decade earlier, had weighed 187 pounds. The plaster of Paris cast of Carnera's hands, once on exhibition at the third Madison Square Garden, is said to be that of the largest fists in boxing history.

Léon See was a hustler and promoter in Paris who learned of Carnera when he was working the circus circuit in France. The deal there was to go two rounds with the giant and win a cash prize. Legend has it that once a guy went into the second round, Carnera would work him across the ring until the mark's back was pinned against a curtain. A fellow behind it would then smite him (unseen, of course) on the back of the head with a 2 × 4. When Carnera left the circus, both he and the 2 × 4 retired undefeated. See put

Carnera on tour in Italy, Germany, France, Spain, and England. It was in England that Friedman saw him, and the rest became a story in search of a mandatory end.

At this time, Jack Dempsey was retired and America was staggering in the first throes of the Great Depression. For both reasons, boxing needed a drawing card, and with Carnera, Owney Madden now controlled the whole damned deck.

Madden launched his new attraction with just two house rules for potential opponents: One, you had to lose. Two, Carnera's opponents had to agree to allow Friedman in their corner as their chief second so he could enforce the terms of the agreement if necessary. This became known as "the Friedman Rule."

In Philly, against a competent but aging Roy Ace Clark, the Friedman Rule first came into play. When Clark decided between rounds that he could win, Friedman shoved two wads of cotton in Clark's nostril. Pulling cotton out of your nose while wearing boxing gloves is not unlike trying to cross the Gobi Desert on ice skates. Roy opened his mouth to breathe, and Carnera hit him and broke his jaw.

Against a fellow named Bombo Chevalier in the Oakland Oaks ballpark in California, a similar scene transpired—but this time Friedman pulled a large gun out of his cardigan sweater pocket and asked, "What do you think, Bombo?" To which Chevalier replied, "I think I am going to lose."

The fact that Carnera won seventeen straight against willing accomplices by knockout should not be surprising. But perhaps the best anecdote comes certified by the aforementioned Willie Gilzenberg. Gilzenberg booked Carnera into the Newark Armory and sold eight thousand seats. He did so because he came up with the perfect gimmick. Not only had nobody seen Carnera throw many punches with bad intentions at the time, they had also never seen Carnera get hit.

Gilzenberg hired a prominent New York trainer named Dumb Dan Morgan. "You will see Carnera hit by Cowboy Billy Owen. I guarantee it," Dumb Dan trumpeted. So they paid, they came, and this is what they saw.

See had told Carnera that, because of his size, nobody would dare hit him. But when Cowboy Billy hit him on the shoulder, Carnera turned to the Italian-American referee, Gene Roman, and said in his native tongue, "He hit me."

"Well," Roman answered in Italian, "I suggest you hit him back."

Cowboy Billy immediately went in the tank as soon as Carnera figured it out.

However, the game was wearing thin—too many no-punch knockouts, too many unexplained knockdowns, too many skeptical newspaper reporters. Madden, therefore, took another one of his heavyweights, Max Baer, who *could* fight, and made the Carnera–Baer fight for the title that Carnera had just won from Jack Sharkey, a fight which Sharkey's wife insisted had been thrown.

Baer dropped Carnera a total of eleven times in eleven rounds to win. Madden then cast his giant in the role of opponent. His last major fight was in that billing, and Joe Louis destroyed him.

Meanwhile, like every mobster who had owned a serious piece of the boxing industry, Madden was hurtling toward the fall from grace. A notorious killer named Mad Dog Coll had been extorting money from Madden and his cohorts. Coll was assassinated in a phone booth while talking to on the phone to, well, Madden. Police could prove nothing, but they began to pressure him and so did other Mafia families squeezing his Greenwich Village turf. In 1935, he quit both boxing and the rackets. He never returned to New York.

Madden was gone, but the mob wasn't about to abdicate its stranglehold on boxing. After all, the two biggest sporting events in America were boxing's championship fights and the World Series. The control of boxing—through fixed fights involving fixed fighters, fixed referees, fixed judges, or all three—only tightened that control. Compliant managers who were either mobbed-up themselves or easily extorted, and promoters who needed to pay homage to the mob in order to get fights, were a big part of the story. It would not be until Sonny Liston lost the heavyweight championship to Muhammad Ali in 1964 that the mob lost its last controlled fighter of stature.

The man whose underworld influence would enable him to control an entire professional sport for decades was named Frankie Carbo, who used the alias of Mr. Gray in some of his business dealings. Unlike Owney Madden, he was not a man about town. He did not mix with New York's elite citizens. What he was instead was a Lucchese crime family "button man," or mafia soldier.

Carbo was a cold-blooded murderer and hit man for higherups in the mob, who also ran his own fiefdom through a chain of other thugs. His trusted lieutenant was a man named Frank "Blinky" Palermo, an associate of the powerful Frank Bruno crime family in Philadelphia, who had an unsavory boxing background even before he met Carbo. To terrified managers, promoters, and fighters, a "suggestion" from Palermo was clearly a message from Carbo. The names of the pair's criminal associates, who served as front men for the enterprise, made up a list long enough to fill much of the nation's police blotters—which they did.

The most serious ally Carbo had was an entrepreneur named James D. Norris, the son of James E. Norris, a millionaire who owned the National Hockey League's New York Rangers. Since the Rangers was one of the Garden's principal tenants, Norris Senior was the largest stockholder of Madison Square Garden. In 1949, Norris Junior would continue to keep the Garden in the family by taking control of it through his corporation, the International Boxing Club of New York (IBC). Norris made a secret agreement with Carbo. He would provide the building and Carbo would provide the fighters, leading to a nefarious relationship in the boxing scene. With both the mob and Norris's backing, an event occurred that illustrated what had become Carbo's long reach as boxing's master puppeteer.

The most respected trainer in boxing at the time was Ray Arcel. Arcel never wanted to manage fighters because he believed his gift was in developing their talents. The idea, however, of promoting their fights appealed to him. Because of his straight-arrow reputation, honest fighters and managers rushed to join him.

Around this time, Carbo already had two highly lucrative televised fight cards with national sponsors. On Wednesday there were the Pabst Blue Ribbon fights, and on Friday the Gillette Friday night fights. When Arcel reasoned that Saturday night was fair game and made his own national TV contract, Carbo was enraged. One Saturday afternoon in Boston, Arcel prepared for one of his fight cards as usual, unaware that Carbo's contract on Arcel had already been accepted by a hit man.

In September 1953, when Arcel left the nearby Manger Hotel to join a group of managers on the sidewalk outside the Boston Gardens Arena, a Carbo emissary named Bill Daly identified a nearby thug when Arcel joined the group. The thug went straight for him with a lead pipe, striking him twice in the head and nearly crushing his skull. Arcel lay on a hospital bed for nineteen days. So long was Carbo's reach that a lifelong friend of Arcel's slept in his hospital room with a loaded gun. Carbo's message was not lost on the boxing industry.

Carbo was the unchallenged brain who ran both Norris and most of boxing as well. His string of murders (with no convictions) was well-known and feared. He surrounded himself with enough added muscle to solidify his claim as the uncrowned czar of American boxing, against underworld challengers and honest citizens alike. Although he controlled Sonny Liston, who would become the "last mob fighter," Carbo found his take far more lucrative among the lightweights, welterweights, and middleweights.

Although Carbo had already performed multiple killings as a button man for New York's Lucchese family and a freelancer for

Murder, Inc., the notorious contract executioners for the mafia during the 1930s, his entry into the boxing business in the 1940s was actually a fortuitous accident.

The story is that none of this might have happened had a Syracuse barber, who knew nothing about boxing, not won the managership of a local fighter in a floating crap game. According to Willie Gilzenberg, the barber was a cousin of one of Carbo's associates. "He ain't too smart about boxing," Gilzenberg said the associate told Carbo. "Do me a favor, will ya? Take that fighter, move him along, and make sure my cousin gets his cut. I'd appreciate it very much."

Within two years, through threats and favors, Carbo had moved his prospect and a lot of other mediocre fighters along. Then he wound up with Eddie Babe Risko, the middleweight champion of the world. That relationship was an ominous signpost of what was yet to come.

Before his wild journey of more than two decades ended, Carbo (and, to a lesser degree, his number one associate, Blinky Palermo) would extort as many as a hundred managers and fighters, fix hundreds of fights, bribe dozens of boxing judges, and turn boxing in general—and the lightweights, welters, and middles in particular—into a personal cash cow.

To understand how it was done, I offer again the testimony of Gilzenberg, who was clearly in a position to know. Gilzenberg, who had earlier been involved in the certification of Primo Carnera for Owney Madden, would meet Carbo for the first time a half decade later in 1935.

On April 12, 1933, Frankie Carbo walked off the elevator on an upper floor at the Carteret Hotel in Elizabeth, New Jersey, and entered a suite shared by bootleggers Max Greenberg and Max Haskell. What followed is somewhat unclear because every witness came down with a remarkable case of amnesia when it came to indictment time. All that can be said with certainty is that the pair had apparently tried to catch a lot of bullets with their stomachs. When the cops arrived they found them just a little bit dead. Two years later in 1935, Carbo was arrested, winding up in the Union County jail for six months (he would later walk away a free man when the cops discovered no witnesses and no gun).

At this time, Gilzenberg, who was managing fighters on his own and promoting fights weekly from a neighborhood fight club, Laurel Garden in Newark, New Jersey, realized he needed a main event for February 1936. Suddenly, with Carbo in jail, the possibility of a fight in February looked a lot brighter for Gilzenberg. Carbo's fighter, Eddie Babe Risko, was due to fight, and the commissions were clamoring to take his title unless he defended it soon. Gilzenberg visited the Union County Jail and asked to see Carbo. Remarkably, he was told by the desk sergeant, "I'll see if he's busy."

Carbo agreed to five minutes. When Gilzenberg was ushered inside, this is what he saw:

"The cell door was opened wide, Carbo was getting a manicure and a uniformed waiter from Newark's only five-star restaurant [The Tavern] was setting a table for his dinner.

"'What the hell do you want?' he demanded. 'I am very busy. You better talk fast.'

"'You are going to lose the middleweight title unless you listen to me. I got a guy named Tony Fisher who your guy will have no trouble beating. Fight him at my joint in Newark and get the boxing officials off your back.'

"'All right. You got it. Now get the hell outta here. Go over to Brooklyn and see Joey A, and tell him Mr. Gray give you the okay.'"

So Gilzenberg went down to a night club on Pineapple Street to see Joey A, better known on assorted police blotters as Joey Adonis.

"I tell him I want to make the Risko–Fisher fight," Gilzenberg reported to me, "and he tells me, 'So make it.'

"So I say, 'Just like that?' and he says, 'Yeah, just like that. Usual rules, of course.'

"'What usual rules?' I ask.

"'Your guy wins, we own him.'

"'When do I get him back?'

"'When your guy loses.'"

Risko won easily by unanimous decision to keep the title.

Carbo rolled on. Years later in 1941, one of his colleagues at Murder, Inc., Abe "Twist" Reles, agreed to testify against Carbo in a separate murder case involving the killing of informant Harry Greenberg in 1939. The cops took Reles into protective custody and stashed him at the Half Moon Hotel in Coney Island on an upper floor with appropriate police protection—they said. Reles and the cop with him shared room service. That night, according to his protector, Reles suddenly tried to reach the ground floor without the benefit of an elevator, a staircase, or a parachute. What was left of him was ruled a suicide. Once again, Carbo was a free man.

Meanwhile, a significant sub-plot involving boxing and the mob was playing out to new heights. It had begun with the valid economic cliché that whoever controlled the heavyweight champion controlled all of boxing, and by extension Madison Square Garden, its stage. First, there had been Tex Rickard, who ran boxing through Jack Dempsey and his manager, Doc Kearns, and who actually built a new and larger Madison Square Garden in 1925. Rickard was also responsible for the first million-dollar fight when Dempsey fought Georges Carpentier in Jersey City.

In 1936, a former ticket scalper named Mike Jacobs, got the right to promote the Joe Louis–James Braddock championship fight. By then, Jacobs was the sole owner of his corporation, the Twentieth Century Sporting Club, which was challenging Madison Square Garden for boxing supremacy. Louis, who was promoted by Jacobs, won, and as a result Jacobs became "the man" at the Garden. It was no accident that the area between the arena and the Hotel Forest (another hangout) soon became known as Jacobs Beach.

It stayed that way until Jacobs had a stroke and was bought out. In search of a man who could restore the building to its traditional boxing stature, the board of directors reached out to James D. Norris. With Louis available, Norris did not need to develop his own heavyweight champ. He had something far better. After a meeting at Kearns's home, with Carbo as well as Louis's friend and Norris's assistant, Truman Gibson, present, Norris formed a new secret and evil partnership.

Norris was president of the International Boxing Club of New York from 1949 to 1958. He ran boxing at the Garden and occasionally elsewhere, with a little help from his new friend Carbo. Part of the deal, which was scrupulously observed, was the agreement that they would never be seen together in public. Gibson would be the go-between. As an addendum to their agreement, a woman named Viola Masters, with no apparent public qualifications but one major private one, received forty-five thousand dollars over a three-year period from Madison Square Garden as a "consultant." Her husband was Frankie Carbo. Viola had never seen a fight.

When Carbo was in town, you could generally find him sitting with a cup of coffee alone at a table in what was then named the Garden Cafeteria. It was catty-corner across Eighth Avenue from Madison Square Garden. On Tuesdays and Thursdays, it was packed with college basketball fans. On Friday nights it was filled by the hungry on their way to fight night at the Garden. On Sundays and Wednesdays, the hockey nuts took over. But on weekdays, rain or shine, it was Mr. Gray's office.

The crowd would come—managers, fighters, and colleagues—to wheel, deal, and seek favors from Carbo. At the same time, the group of "soldiers" in his Queensbury Army grew exponentially through the 1940s and 1950s. His network of managers and fighters ran from Boston to Florida to California, with stops in between in New York, Newark, Houston, New Orleans, Chicago, Detroit,

St. Louis, and Denver. Whenever Frankie Carbo offered a "suggestion," no matter where he was, willing ears reacted with the speed of Pavlov's dog.

His was a government that demanded total loyalty. His secretary of state was the Philadelphia numbers king, Blinky Palermo. Unlike the other spiders in his web, Palermo was more partner than employee. According to the late Jim Murray, Pulitzer Prize–winning sports columnist of the *Los Angeles Times*, "Blinky got his nickname because he could never look any man in the eye, including the half-dozen or so who accused him of murder. Blinky was a very rough customer; if you didn't think so, go dig through the dumps or drag the rivers around his native Philadelphia."

Theirs was a marriage made in purgatory, lasting until their ultimate incarceration in separate prisons. Even afterward, it is said that Viola Masters's checks from Madison Square Garden kept coming. Among fighters openly—or, more often, secretly—under contract to Palermo and, therefore, by osmosis to Carbo, were welterweight champions Virgil Akins and Johnny Saxton, lightweight champ Ike Williams, heavyweight contender Coley Wallace, another welterweight champ, Kid Gavilan, and he of proven fixed-fight fame, Black Jack Billy Fox. Fox, who won thirty-six straight fights at the start of his career—all by knockout—was matched with Jake LaMotta in 1947 at Carbo's "suggestion." Thus, Carbo and Palermo set the stage to cash in on a huge betting coup when they got LaMotta to throw the fight, a fact later confirmed before a Congressional committee. LaMotta was rewarded down the line with a shot at Marcel Cerdan's middleweight title fight, which he won when the Frenchman's shoulder was dislocated during a LaMotta-inspired wrestling sequence.

And so it went. Some fights were fixed, as were some judges. Some fights were spectacular because Carbo owned both fighters; he knew their styles and wanted to set up a match he knew he couldn't lose. The Republic of Carbo, the International

Boxing Club (in this case, synonymous with Madison Square Garden), and affiliated subjects never had cause to blink. It made money; cashed couldn't-lose bets; and owned titles, fighters, and judges.

One rarely discussed but classic example of Carbo's versatility in pulling the strings surfaced years later, when insiders discussed the Marciano–Walcott heavyweight championship fight in Philadelphia in 1952. Marciano was managed by Al Weil, a former IBC matchmaker who, as a manager, was safely in the Carbo group. Walcott was managed by Felix Boccichio, whose connection to Mr. Gray was well known. What was not known was that Carbo actually put together the contracts.

It is remembered as one of the great heavyweight fights of all time, and why not? Carbo knew boxing. He had a piece of both fighters. He couldn't lose. Free of any interfering by him, the two fought brilliantly. As blood streamed from a cut above Marciano's eye, both men threw right hands thirty seconds into the thirteenth round— but Marciano's got there first. Walcott couldn't beat the count after it dropped him, and the heavyweight title changed hands.

Carbo was thrilled. He had seen a great fight, and even though a new champion had come out of it, Mr. Gray still very much had a piece of the heavyweight championship. Life was good in the Republic of Carbo. Only one guy could screw it up.

His name was Frankie Carbo. And he did.

When his empire suddenly collapsed without warning, it wasn't an issue of inefficiency; and it wasn't miscalculation that forged the beginning of the end. It was the blind, stubborn greed of both Carbo and Palermo, combined with the kind of stupidity that, until then, had never caught up with them. It involved the kind of egos that never knew enough to walk away from a deal gone bad.

It began with the same kind of scenario that had never backfired before. Don Jordan was a welterweight of erratic but often effective skill who fought primarily on the West Coast. In terms of managers who could make a major deal for him, he wasn't getting much help. His manager, Don Nesseth, had come late to boxing. A local car dealer, Nesseth was far more fan than boxing professional. Don Chargin, who promoted on his own in Oakland and who had a small piece of Jordan's contract, told me that Nesseth was not "connected." "He was just a good guy, straight-arrow honest, and a fellow who wanted to do the best he could for his fighters."

Nesseth realized he needed the right introduction to get a title shot for his fighter. To that end, he asked Jackie Leonard, the matchmaker at the Hollywood Legion, to approach Truman Gibson, Norris, and Carbo for help. In record time, Jordan was matched with hard-punching Virgil Akins, the welterweight champion.

There had not been much to recommend Jordan behind his team's cry for help. Outside the ring he was even more erratic. He had been arrested for assaulting two women with a bow and arrow. He had also been busted for a marijuana violation. Against Akins, he was a heavy underdog. Amazingly, he beat him not once but twice, the second time in Akins's hometown of St. Louis.

Suddenly, a tarnished welterweight star was born.

Even before the rematch, Jordan had gotten Truman Gibson's attention. The front man for Norris (and, therefore, the mob), Gibson had earlier told the Jordan group, according to Chargin, "Look, I wouldn't worry if I were you. If he loses the rematch, and he probably will, nobody will say anything. If he wins, well, then you could be in trouble." Gibson wanted money. Carbo wanted money. Palermo wanted money. And, in its warped sense of honor, the Carbo group actually thought it was the victim, not the victimizer.

"In their eyes," Chargin said, "they had a deal because of a tactical error Leonard made. As the matchmaker, he could not speak for either Jordan or Nesseth. When Gibson said, 'This is what's going to happen. Do you understand?' Leonard did not say yes. He did not say no. Based on the mob's proven winning streak, Carbo took silence to mean acquiescence."

When Jordan beat Akin a second time, the Jordan camp celebrated with a party in matchmaker Jackie Leonard's room at the Chase-Park Plaza Hotel in St. Louis. Then, there was a knock on the door. When Leonard opened it, he was face-to-face with Blinky Palermo.

"I came to see my fighter," Palermo said.

Somebody—Chargin does not remember who—replied, "He ain't your fighter." Later that night, as Chargin and Leonard took a last drink, the phone rang. It was Carbo. "He kept on shouting that a deal is a deal. He shouted a lot worse curse words, but I can't recall them exactly so many years later."

And then the messengers began to call on Leonard. The first was Bill Daly.

"Mr. Gray is angry, and when he gets angry people get hurt—which means dead."

Daly warned Leonard in detail about the consequences: "See what they do, they use a water pipe, see. You know, regular lead pipe. They just get an ordinary piece of newspaper [because it] don't show fingerprints. They give you two bats [with it] . . . try to kill you . . . then drop it in the street and walk away."

Daly did not know that Leonard had taped the whole thing using a wire recording device in partnership with the Los Angeles Police Department. Jim Henderson, then the head of the LA Police intelligence department, was his handler.

Gibson was demanding money. Carbo was demanding his piece of the title. And two local thugs, Joe Di Sica and Tom Dragna, were demanding Leonard convince Nesseth to give in. In another meeting, they had told him to "go kick the shit outta Nesseth or you are out of options." Leonard had already been threatened early on by Di Sica because the Carbo group thought he had something to do with

Nesseth's intransigence, although he did not. Di Sica had whispered in Leonard's ear, "You are in it, Jackie. It's you or Nesseth."

Meanwhile, Leonard's concern was heightened by a phone call from Carbo, as he later testified in court when the five thugs went on trial. Carbo's call went like this: "You son of a bitchin' doublecrosser. You are no good. Your word is no good. Nothing is good about you. Just because you are two thousand miles away is no sign I can't have punks like you taken care of."

In a second telephone call he added, "If I was there, I'd gouge your eyes out. We are going to meet at the cross roads. You will never get away with it. I've had this title for twenty-five years, and no punks like you are going to take it away from me. What I mean [when I say I'll get you] is you're gonna be dead. We will have somebody out there take care of you."

Shortly thereafter, Leonard drove home one evening, opened his garage door, and was immediately and ferociously assaulted. The attackers were pros who only cut short their ambush when Leonard's wife heard the commotion, turned on the outside lights, and began to scream. The interruption saved her husband's life. By then, Leonard was unconscious. Hospitalized, he waged a frightening battle for his life and made it.

These same tactics had always worked in the past, but this time, there were three Leonard tapes and Daly, who had cooperated to save his skin and remained an unindicted co-conspirator. There was also the testimony of Chargin. Leonard had tried to borrow money from the Oakland promoter in order to save his failing club. Later at trial, Chargin told the court he had received an anonymous phone call warning him to "stay out of Hollywood" (in effect warning him not to bail out Leonard). Never once did the Carbo group display the slightest bit of caution. After all, hadn't they always won?

Carbo had ranted and raved that West Coast connections with Jordan had betrayed him when, in fact, the only person who could have brought it all crashing down was himself. The truth was, Jordan was a decent but not spectacular fighter. All Carbo had to do was wait and the title would have ultimately come back to him the first time Jordan lost.

The old movie cliché that Hollywood puts in a mafioso's mouth before he kills a guy—"Don't take it personally, it's only business"— was pure fraud when it came to Carbo. In the moment of truth, for Carbo it was not "just business"; it was "all about ego."

He alone blew the whole deal.

First came the Kefauver hearings in 1950, a special committee of the United States Senate that investigated the organized crime and mob (Cosa Nostra) infiltration of boxing. Carbo took the Fifth Amendment twenty-five times. Palermo also hid behind the Fifth. The hearings morphed into America's universal television entertainment while they lasted.

In 1961, Palermo, Carbo, Di Sica, Dragna, and Gibson were tried on the Jordan case. The trial lasted three months. The attorney general, Robert Kennedy, was the prosecuting attorney. Carbo got twenty-five years, Palermo fifteen, Di Sica and Dragna lesser sentences, and Gibson drew probation. Norris resigned from the Garden, and the Feds dismantled the IBC for violation of the Sherman Anti-Trust Act.

The mob was dead as far as boxing was concerned.

Well, not exactly. The mob had one piece of unfinished boxing business still in its grasp. The last mob fighter was a heavyweight, and he was about to win the world championship. Ironically, because of him and the way he subsequently surrendered it, the greatest and most honest heavyweight era in the history of boxing was on its way.

TWO

The Gatekeeper

"Floyd (Patterson) tells me, 'I will try my best against
Mr. Liston.' Mr. Liston? It's a goddamn fight and all he
can say is he will try his best. He should say he'll tear his
head off. No way is a guy who calls the other guy mister
going to win anything. I just bet Sonny—big."

—*Sid Wyman, president of the Dunes Hotel,
two days before Liston–Patterson II*

It was a time when the heavyweight championship was consigned
to the shadows. No longer was the heavyweight champion of the
world considered the "baddest man" on the planet. Since trainer and
manager Cus D'Amato had steered Floyd Patterson into the championship in 1956, the fighter was better described as the most invisible
man on the planet. It was as though the legacies of Joe Louis, Ezzard
Charles, and Rocky Marciano had slipped through a time warp in
what threatened to be a redundant state of limbo.

When Rocky Marciano retired and Patterson defeated Archie Moore in a box-off for the championship title, the mob was suddenly faced with an unhappy prospect. Al Weil, Marciano's manager, was locked into the mob-friendly confines of Carbo and Norris. Doc Kearns, Moore's manager, was a brilliant but compliant member of the Carbo social set. Now, each had no champion. Dealing with Cus D'Amato was a far different matter.

D'Amato was shrewd, stubborn, and suspicious—an amateur psychologist and paranoiac. He trusted virtually nobody. "Everyone," he told his fighters, "has a weakness." He once told me: "A fighter who has fear and learns to control it can conquer anything. A fighter who has no fear isn't ahead of the game. He is simply crazy."

D'Amato went to war with Madison Square Garden. The Garden, he reasoned, was Carbo. "I will not contaminate my fighters. We will not fight for the mob." He felt he was constantly being stalked by the Carbo–Norris–Palermo axis.

"Once," Don Chargin, the old West Coast matchmaker and promoter, told me, "because the mob-affiliated managers guild was based on the East Coast, D'Amato was trying to romance West Coast managers and fighters. He was in Indianapolis where Floyd Patterson was fighting Brian London, and Cus told me to meet him at his hotel on the Fair Grounds at 11 p.m. So I went and found him living in a room about the size of a broom closet with a small cot, a can of sardines, and box of crackers. I said, 'Let's go out to eat,' and he told me he couldn't because 'they' were trying to poison him. That's how off the wall he was."

D'Amato once had a Puerto Rican middleweight named Jose Torres. Torres could have been one of the great middleweights of his time, but he never had the chance. D'Amato wouldn't match him with the great middleweights because, according to him, that would mean surrendering to the mob. When D'Amato retired, Torres was already past his prime. He wound up winning the light heavyweight championship when he was no longer the great fighter he had been as a middleweight.

As a preteen, Floyd Patterson was shy and reticent to the point of having emotional problems. After he won his championship, he confided to *New York Post* columnist Milt Gross that when faced with any crisis as an elementary school student, he would hide inside a large New York City Transit Authority tool box he discovered in a nearby subway station. He was an introverted loner, and repeated truancy and petty theft resulted in his being sent from his Brooklyn home to the upstate Wiltwyck School for Boys, a reform school.

That's where Cus D'Amato found him.

After Patterson won his elimination bout against Archie Moore on November 30, 1956 (and with it, the heavyweight title), D'Amato fed Patterson a diet of never-were and never-could-be contenders—people like Brian London, a journeyman from England; overrated Roy Harris of Cut and Shoot, Texas; and the active but light-punching Tommy Hurricane Jackson.

Wrapped in the guise of fighting what he trumpeted as his war against the mob, D'Amato would duck every qualified opponent of merit, choose suspect promoters at times, and isolate the heavyweight title from anyone with the slightest chance of beating his fighter. The very first title defense was against Olympic Champion Pete Rademacher, who had never had a professional fight.

The only time D'Amato got fooled was when he found Ingemar Johansson and brought him in from Sweden. It cost him dearly. Johansson knocked Patterson down seven times with his right hand, which Johansson called the Hammer Thor, before referee Ruby Goldstein stopped the fight in the third round. Fortunately for Patterson, he won two exciting rematches by knockout. But one thing was clear. Floyd Patterson was a fighter with the hand speed of an automatic punch press—but the chin of a romantic poet.

Meanwhile, a fighter who represented Cus D'Amato's worst nightmare was already on the way toward humiliating D'Amato's fighter and prying out of the manager's grasp the prize he had hidden away for so long. His name was Charles Sonny Liston. Just two months before Johansson's multiple knockdowns of Patterson during their first fight in June 1959, Liston was beginning to make a case that the public would not let D'Amato avoid. He had won his last sixteen fights, twelve by knockout. Soon, he would step into a ring in Houston, Texas, where he would present major evidence that he was a guy Cus should not let Patterson fight.

On April 15, 1959, Liston would face a man who had the body of a sculpture (he had, indeed, modeled) and a tremendous right hand. Liston engendered the feeling among reporters that to fight Cleveland Williams was to go to war. That night, Liston proved he had something Patterson in no way could match: it was Liston's chin, which Williams tested ferociously in the very first round. One right hand damn near knocked Liston out of the ring.

In the third, Liston came out calmly and put Williams down first for an eight-count, and then finished him at 2:13. Everyone who saw the earlier onslaught Liston had survived was convinced that here was the next heavyweight champion—if he could get Patterson into the same ring with him.

Meanwhile, D'Amato continued in his role as self-proclaimed crime fighter, telling all who would listen that he was the standard bearer for an all-out war against the mob that had infiltrated boxing. However, which mob was he referring to? The truth was, to call D'Amato a crime fighter would be total fiction. He was himself tied to a mobster by the name of Fat Tony Salerno. When foreign fighters came over to the United States to challenge Patterson, they needed an American representative. Interestingly enough, a fellow named Charles Black filled the role at the suggestion of D'Amato. In fact, his name wasn't really Black; it was Charles Antonucci, and Charles's cousin was Fat Tony Salerno, the man who ran the numbers racket in Harlem and who rose to become the boss of the two-hundred-member Genovese Family. An investigation into boxing racketeering in New York would later prove that, while Bill Rosenson might have been listed as the promoter of record for the first Ingemar Johansson fight, the bout was actually underwritten by Fat Tony.

Despite this, D'Amato continued to cast himself as crime fighter, taking advantage of that alleged role to feed Patterson a number of non-entities. All the while, top contenders like Eddie Machen and Zora Foley, though not "connected," were flat out ducked. Patterson was the good soldier, fighting whenever, wherever, and whomever D'Amato selected. It was easy for him to remain above the fray. He was introverted, self-conscious, and low on self-esteem, even though he had one hell of a fast pair of hands. It never occurred to him that the biggest, baddest mob-owned fighter of them all, Sonny Liston, was being deliberately avoided by D'Amato. D'Amato knew full well that Patterson could not have beaten Liston with a gun, a whip, and a chair, so he kept Patterson safely tucked out of harm's way.

Who exactly was Sonny Liston, and what were the forces that shaped both him and his relationship with the mob? For starters, he was the product of the kind of poverty generally reserved for Great Depression novels. His father, Tobe Liston, married twice and sired twenty-five children. Sonny was the twenty-fourth child. The old man was a tenant farmer, and his use of domestic violence was so protracted that Sonny's mother left, taking a few of the kids with her. Sonny remained to work the field as a pre-teen. Allegedly, in one story, when his father's mule died, Sonny was made to pull the plough. The beatings from his father for family infractions were so severe that Sonny claimed the scars were still visible on his back decades later. At age thirteen, he ran away to St. Louis to join his mother.

Education was hopeless. He had none back in Arkansas and almost none in St. Louis. A series of armed robberies followed, and Liston was sentenced to five years in the Missouri State Penitentiary in 1950, around the age of twenty. It was there that Father Alois Stevens started him in boxing, which led to his early parole. in 1952 Liston signed a professional contract a year later. At the same time, he found work as an enforcer for a local mobster, but it did not prevent him from launching his career as a boxer. He won five straight, and then surprised a national television audience by winning a decision over ranked John Summerlin (18–1–1) in his opponent's hometown of Detroit. He kept winning until, in May of 1956, a cop confronted him about a cab parked near Liston's home. The issue was never clear. Liston broke the officer's knee, shattered a piece of his face, and fought with a quartet of backup police who repeatedly hit him flush on the skull with nightsticks—and still had trouble putting him on the ground. It drew a nine-month jail term.

When he finally came out, both his in-the-ring and out-of-it activities continued in the same way. The arrests mounted up. The St. Louis cops had painted an invisible target on his back, and they kept hitting bull's-eyes.

It was 1958. Bernie Glickman, a front for the Chicago mob, had Liston in a main event in the Windy City against Billy Hunter. When Liston knocked out Hunter in four, he attracted the undivided attention of Carbo, Palermo, and other family heads who had supported the pair. The next day, according to author Nick Tosches, Glickman received a phone call from Sam Giancana, a Chicago mob boss who, in effect, told Glickman he could neither manage nor promote Liston. That would fall to the St. Louis mobster Pep Barone. Glickman was told he would be paid seventy-three thousand dollars to step aside, which he did. Meanwhile, Liston had gone from victimizer to police victim. The war between Liston and the police continued at a furious pace. A local police official told him to "get out of St. Louis or you will be found dead one day in an alley."

When Barone moved to Philadelphia, Palermo's hometown, Liston followed. In the ring, Liston was unstoppable. Genuine contenders fell by the roadside: Cleveland Williams, Willi Bes-manoff, Roy Harris, Zora Foley, Eddie Machen. It is worth noting that while Liston knocked out Roy Harris in just one round, it took Patterson twelve rounds to do the same job. Along with that success, Liston simultaneously drew the undivided attention of Philadelphia Police Commissioner (and later two-term mayor) Frank Rizzo. His police were unrelenting in their crusade against Liston after obvious hints from their boss. Liston made it easy with public displays of drunken behavior.

There were serious doubts as to whether the mob could deliver the title fight against Floyd Patterson. The National Association for the Advancement of Colored People (NAACP) was against it (Liston was a terrible role model, they said). President John F. Kennedy was against it. To that end, when Patterson visited the White House, Kennedy showed him a report from the Justice Department citing Liston's ties to the mob and asked him to avoid the fight. The American public wasn't too wild about that idea. Heavyweight boxer Jack Dempsey also said that Liston should not be allowed to fight, citing the same reasons. Liston responded by asking Dempsey to explain why he took a deferment to work in a defense plant rather than enlist in the army. (Ironically, Dempsey's old manager, Doc Kearns, had his own cozy accommodation with the IBC and the Carbo group, with the Marciano–Walcott fight as a prime example.)

But a heavyweight is a heavyweight is a heavyweight, and it was becoming the opinion of boxing aficionados everywhere that if you looked up the word *heavyweight* in any dictionary, you expected to find Sonny Liston's picture next to it. When the Kefauver Committee told Liston they believed he was a 100 percent mob fighter, he told them he had a new manager, George Katz. Katz was a Philadelphia fight manager with a pristine reputation. How the mob permitted this wasn't clear, but while Katz was Liston's manager, they knew they could still force their way into a piece of the action after he won the title.

And then there was the "Floyd factor." Stung by the underground telegraph whispers that he was afraid of Liston, Patterson finally told D'Amato he would fight Liston—with or without him.

The fight was signed for September 25, 1962, at the Chicago White Sox's Comiskey Park. The fighters trained twenty miles apart. Liston was at an abandoned harness track in suburban Aurora, where the weeds in the infield were as high as an elephant's eye, and unseasonable dishwater-gray clouds hung over the disused oval like the promise of the storm Sonny's fists could create. The venue was as charming as the municipal dumps.

Patterson's camp was in the pastoral hills of a place called Marycrest Farm. The first day I went to see him, I saw a family of little bunnies hop across the road. I wondered whether the two training sites were an outdoor ad for premonitions.

The tension between D'Amato and his fighter was palpable. In all previous such situations, they had either shared quarters or been a hop and a jump from each other. But this time Patterson was at the top of a hill and D'Amato was at the bottom. They did not speak to each other much.

D'Amato's new role had morphed into a kind of modern day sweat-shirted Diogenes, a man who lived for the truth as he saw it while talking your ear off explaining it.

"The promoters," he told us, "are blaming us for what they are doing to Liston [who would fight for a paltry 12 percent of the spoils]. They are using Floyd, too, because the bulk of the money goes to them. People blame me for everything. Someday, I'll write a book and they'll know the truth. I opposed this fight. I oppose it now, and you know why [a sly reference to his self-appointed role as Cus the crimefighter]." After each statement that followed, he would append the words, "and you know why." After twenty minutes, those in the audience began to nod their heads at the phrase, which none of them really understood. D'Amato could do that to you.

"We never ducked anybody. It was Hitler who said that if you repeat a lie over and over, people will believe it [in fact, the quote is attributed to Joseph Goebbels]. That's what they are doing—and you know who they are. But I'm not worried. Floyd Patterson will win this fight. He will not be intimidated by this man."

An hour later, at the top of the hill, Patterson held court. "I never fought anyone who looks as big as Liston. I have no plan and no strategy. But I will know what to do. I am the champion."

I recalled thinking as I left, *But for how long?*

To get to Liston's camp, you had to slog your way across the infield and through the weeds, which swayed in the wind like something that belonged in the Mato Grosso. Then you walked down the cold stone concrete corridor, underneath the grandstand, and into an unpainted former storeroom. The ring was about the size of five postage stamps. A rope stretched at an angle between several seats and the rest of the room. Geraldine Liston, Sonny's wife, sat there alone. When I approached her to see if we could talk, a hand carrying the weight of the entire Green Bay Packers linebacking corps seemed to press down on my shoulder from behind.

It was Himself.

"This side is for her. You go over there."

I didn't salute—but I thought about it.

I moved into a seat next to Jack Nilon, Liston's new manager. Without so much as an announcement, Nilon and his brother, who were partners in stadium and arena food concessions in Philly, had bought an interest in Liston's contract. The press used to call Liston's old manager, George Katz, "Mr. Clean," a nickname he earned from the Kefauver Committee when he would testify that he was clean. Now, Mr. Clean had been replaced by twin hotdog vendors.

Nilon was a manager without a license. "This is my first fight," he told me. He was a financial advisor who had no money to invest for his fighter because Liston had yet to earn a dime under him.

"Do you have a contract with him?" I ask.

"I have an understanding."

"Do you get a salary or, perhaps, a commission?"

"I don't get a salary or a commission."

I almost added, "No wonder the mob let you in." But I didn't.

With that, Liston bounded into the ring wearing a hooded Turkish towel bathrobe. It was the kind of robe a freshly bathed four-year-old kid might have worn without the hood—if he weighed 212 pounds. He shadowboxed. Then he banged away at a heavy bag until a left hook knocked it loose from its anchor. He took a series of medicine balls in his gut as a loudspeaker played "Night Train." Finally, he jumped rope. During this last exercise routine, you could almost imagine him chanting a variation of the old schoolyard litany:

S, my name is Sonny. I came from St. Louis and I smash jawbones.

Then he sat for questions, just as Joe Louis walked in. "Was Joe your boyhood idol?" someone asked. "Do you get a charge out of seeing him?"

"Why?" Liston shot back. "He ain't gonna win the fight for me."

Bob Montgomery, once a great lightweight, was also there as Liston's guest. When asked who would win, he paused, tapped his chin, and said, "The fight will be won here." The implication was that Patterson's chin had the consistency of Dresden china.

"Well, how you gonna cope with Floyd's speed?" another guy asked Liston.

"What speed?" Liston replied. "Can he run like Billy Conn? What makes him so fast? You saw him catch a bullet?"

I had the distinct feeling, thinking about both camps, that a mood had been set here.

It was four days before the fight. Out in Aurora, Liston listened to jazz records like "You Beat Me to the Punch." The rest of the time, he whacked the heavy bag off its chain, caught a medicine ball in his gut without so much as a grunt, and snarled at one of his retinue to get him a towel.

Meanwhile, over at the farm, Patterson spoke softly, in a friendly tone. "You know when I'm knocked down," he said, "I don't acknowledge the referee counting. The only thing in my mind is to get up, and that might happen again. I am the champion. It would be greed to ask for more. I believe I can take a punch as well as any heavyweight. I am the only man, however, who believes it."

He would neither praise nor pan Liston. He simply said he would retain his title. D'Amato added, "You all know that there were people who wanted this fight because I didn't want it. They had reasons of their own, and you know who they are and you know why."

Patterson was confident; so was D'Amato. So why was it that, as I drove back to Chicago, the strains of "Night Train" kept rattling around in my brain?

All week long, the giant screen at press headquarters in Chicago's Sheraton Hotel had been a thunderous montage of the life and times of Floyd Patterson. It was an active piece of propaganda during which Patterson sends nineteen bodies to the canvas in thirty-two minutes. It all happens so fast that the only thing missing is the clown car with the Keystone Kops.

As a public service, the promoters loaned Sonny Liston a copy of the film. He checked into a local hotel the night before the fight and watched it from start to finish, then yawned and promptly fell asleep with sweet dreams of how this would be no contest.

At the weigh-in the next morning, Liston proceeded to stare Patterson into what looked like a near-comatose state. At 9:30 p.m. that night, he lumbered into the ring and never took his eyes off Patterson, who sat drawn and docile on his stool, eyes averted.

There was the kind of bravado born of desperation in his corner. D'Amato gave his fighter a quick handshake. At the bell, Danny Florio, the cutman, began hollering advice: "Hand up, baby . . . do it . . . move . . . do it, baby . . . hands up."

Across the way, Liston's corner said nothing. It had learned over the sullen training period that Sonny asks for no advice, takes none, and, perhaps, needs none.

It was simply three left hooks from Liston that hurt the fragile hope of law and order. Soon after, a looping right hurt Patterson again. The nation might have been rooting hard for Patterson, but in boxing it is axiomatic that idols with glass jaws become idols with clay feet. Liston threw the left hook. It rattled crockery, it crossed eyes, and it ended the fight. It had taken Liston just two minutes and six seconds into the very first round to take the heavyweight championship of the planet.

Referee Frank Sikora supported Patterson as his wife rushed into the ring. Liston, meanwhile, stood tall and wide like a building inspector studying what was left of the building whose implosion he had just supervised. Liston was caught from behind in a wild rush by his trainer, Willie Reddish; his cutman, Joe Polino; and his manager of record, Jack Nilon. The final bizarre touch came as two policemen were helping Patterson toward his dressing room—the Comiskey Park organist broke into a rousing chorus of "Chicago, Chicago." It was apt, since New York and California had refused the match and Philadelphia, Liston's new hometown, had been ruled out by the Patterson camp.

In the dressing room afterward, Liston explained, "The first two times the referee says, 'Break,' and he does. When he doesn't the third time, I think he's hurt.

"After I hit him another left, I know he's hurt. Then I hit him with one last round, and it's over."

It was at that point that Floyd Patterson slumped liquidly to the floor. The entire exercise took less time than you'd need to hard boil an egg. Liston's remarks were gracious. Suddenly, he was a man who couldn't wait to go home and soak up the new love he was sure America was about to shower on him.

Jack McKinney, a Philadelphia sportswriter and friend of mine, shared the flight home with him two days later. "Sonny couldn't wait to see the crowd that would greet him," he told me. "He had actually written a speech."

It was a speech he never delivered. Liston dreamt of hosting a celebration that would never happen. When he landed, there was nobody present but a handful of reporters. He never got over it. Rizzo's police force had targeted him and, in truth, his behavior made it easy for them. He drank heavily. It was almost inevitable that he would soon leave town. Denver, for a time, would be his new home. His first statement upon arrival was: "I'd rather be a lamp post in Denver than the mayor of Philadelphia."

The contract called for a rematch with Patterson, but there was only one obstacle. When Miami Beach was announced as the site, a strange thing changed their minds: nobody seemed to care. That became clear the moment tickets went on sale, but by then both men had already set up their training camps—Patterson at Hialeah Park Race Track, and Liston at a small kosher hotel called the Casablanca, just off Collins Avenue.

Hialeah was a tough place to find. Depending on where you came from, you might have had to change highways twice. But two thousand people showed up the day Patterson opened camp. The next day, I stopped by the Casablanca to see Liston train. A ring had been set up by the pool. By actual count there were seven people there to watch Liston and, as he boxed, the loudspeaker system kept advertising cha cha lessons in the lounge.

I hung around and waited for Liston to come out. He did not know I was coming, and he had hardly been hospitable back at Aurora Downs. Then I noticed Geraldine Liston sitting facing the ocean.

"Mrs. Liston," I said, "I don't know if you remember me, but in Aurora . . ."

"Yes, I do, and Charles was very rude to you there. Sit down. You will get your interview."

The next thing I knew, he was standing in front of me glaring at his wife. She said, "Don't be rude, Charles. This man is going to get the interview he should have gotten in Illinois."

A thundercloud seemed to cross his face as he stared silently at me. Then he said, perhaps to save face, "You can stay, but that pipe you smokin' got to go."

I immediately threw it in the ocean.

I remarked that two thousand people had come to watch Patterson and only seven were there for him. I asked what he thought about it.

He stared and stared, and said nothing. Fortunately, I said nothing back. Finally, he said, "If this be the olden days when the tribe follow the chief into battle, I be scared." He laughed and added, "Maybe this fight be shorter than the first one."

Two weeks later, with the box office ailing, Liston ailed too. He claimed he had a bad back, and since they had yet to invent the MRI, nervous promoters postponed the fight and moved it to Las Vegas.

Vegas is a place where nobody knows what time it is because the clickety-click of dice on green felt tables respects no hour. There are no clocks in the casinos and no daylight streaming into the rooms. There is no afternoon, no concept of tonight or tomorrow. A dealer on the lam from Louisiana once told me, "In this joint, it's like you're working on a submarine. There is only now."

It was, therefore, the best possible place for Floyd Patterson not to think about what lay ahead.

The whole history of Liston and Patterson had encompassed just 126 seconds—until now, leading up to fight night on July 22, 1963. The more one thinks about what happened in Chicago, the more they are convinced that Patterson is playing Willie Loman in Arthur

Miller's play *Death of a Salesman*, trying to make one last sale that is always a light year away.

Sid Wyman, a "connected" Vegas pioneer, was the final word on everything at the Dunes Hotel, where Patterson was staying. Two days before the fight, he asked Patterson if he could win. He replied, "I will try my best against Mr. Liston."

"Mr. Liston," Wyman recounted, when he told me the story. "Mr. Liston? It's a goddamn fight and all he can say is he will try his best. He should say he'll tear his head off. No way is a guy who calls the other guy *mister* going to win anything. I went out and bet the farm on Sonny. I had to give 4–1, and after what I heard from Floyd, I didn't even blink."

Sports betting in Vegas back then in no way reflects the massive industry it has now become. According to Jimmy Vaccaro, the chief oddsmaker at South Point Hotel and Casino in those days, "There was a tacit agreement between legal bookie joints and the casinos that we wouldn't make any book if they wouldn't have any slot machines. So in those days you had the Rose Bowl, the Santa Anita, and the Hialeah Turf Club, legal joints that did nothing but make book. Then the casinos woke up and took it all over."

The week of Liston–Patterson II, I ran a quick survey of the odds on the fight in Vegas bookie joints. At the Hialeah, a guy named Bobby who was behind the counter said that his guys made Liston a 3–1 choice. However, he added the disclaimer: "It could be 4–1 or 50–1 because we are getting absolutely no action. I can tell you for sure that whatever we win I ain't gonna be able to retire off it. They are betting," he said, with obvious disdain, "only twenty or thirty bucks a pop."

Over at the Santa Anita, Jasper, the oddsmaker, said, "Most all of the money is on which round it will end, and most of those bets are Sonny very early. This fight will be over so quick that they can have dinner and still make the show over at the Sands."

This notion was in no way discredited when Patterson confessed to the media that he still had the fake beard and sunglasses that he wore to get out of town after the Chicago nightmare. When told of this, Liston grunted and said, "Good. I'll give him a chance to wear them both. How long was the first fight?" Liston paused, grunted, and said, "Could be shorter this time."

And so it went, that week in Vegas without drama, without a great deal of money, and without much excitement. That is, until later in the week when Las Vegas, Nevada, got to meet a man named Cassius Marcellus Clay.

I had casually known Clay when he won an Olympic gold medal as the light heavyweight boxing champion in the 1960 Games. I got to know him a little better telephonically when, at the urging of his trainer, Angelo Dundee, he began calling me from such various cultural crossroads as Louisville, Pittsburgh, and Miami Beach, reciting childish poetry and telling me to come to wherever he was fighting and watch it.

I kept telling myself there was no hurry.

But now, Clay was in Las Vegas, roaming the halls of hotels where he was most likely to get in Liston's face—The Thunderbird, The Dunes, and The Stardust. "Hey, bully, fight me," he would challenge. "I will cage the Big Bear," he said. "You ain't nothin'."

All of this was mild entertainment for the tourists, until the day he sneaked up behind Liston at one of the blackjack tables and hollered it all in his ear.

Liston turned halfway in his chair and slapped him. Clay stepped back with a puzzled look on his face and mumbled, "Why did you do that? I'm just tryin' to make you and me a lot of money." Liston turned his head back toward the table and motioned the dealer for another card.

It was finally fight night, and it made Bobby at the Hialeah, Jasper at the Santa Anita, and Liston, who knew it all along, the three smartest men in Sin City. They were right on all counts. It was all over in time for a late dinner and show at the hotel of the customers' choosing.

The beginning of the end came even as a right hand crashed against Floyd Patterson's mouth. It was delivered with the sound a rush of air makes as it sweeps down an empty hallway. It served as traveling music as Patterson stiffened, and when he collapsed it morphed into the sound of mourning, the grudging admission that some seven thousand or so people who gathered in the Las Vegas Convention Center had just paid their way into a wake.

Liston hurt him at the end of a shuffling, sullen walk, the walk that had done the job for him in Chicago a year earlier. Liston was the blue collar guy, carrying the same lunch pail to the same plant, mechanically doing the same job in the same way.

Earlier in the week, Patterson had said, "I could plan my fight, but I have no control over what my mind will do if he hurts me." At the opening bell, Liston came out to meet him and the former champion did a quick dance in retreat. Somebody in his corner hollered, "Stick and run, Floyd!" and he skipped away again as Liston shuffled forward and backed him toward a corner. Liston landed a left against Patterson's head, then threw a right to the mouth and the crowd that had earlier cheered Patterson's entry into the ring and shouted encouragements let out a soft groan, much like a massive vacuum sucking in air. There came another left, and then a crushing right as Patterson sagged to the canvas.

For all intents and purposes, the fight was over, although there followed two more obligatory trips to the canvas before they counted the final ten. Patterson sank to the floor slowly. At the count of seven, he was sitting. At nine, he was on one knee. It was as far as he got. When the referee, Harry Krause, a full-time dealer on the Strip by vocation, counted ten, Liston put his arms around Patterson as he staggered to his feet.

It was over at 2:10 of the first, even before the cigar smoke in the arena had time to form a heavy layer over ringside.

In the end, the week had been good for the town. It brought the high rollers in for the fight. It generated acres of newsprint and miles of TV and radio. It was a financial bonanza for Vegas and a marvelous payday for the champ.

It was, however, a lousy fight.

It was so bad that when Cassius Marcellus Clay vaulted into the ring demanding the inevitable fight with Liston, the crowd bellowed their approval, which is what you'd expect when seven thousand marks who were here to see a fight were instead plucked, fleeced, and otherwise bilked.

Afterward, as the lights went down and the crowd headed for the casinos, Krause shook his head and told the media, "It didn't matter whether he got up or not. I was going to stop it."

The post-fight press conferences were short and to the point. Patterson said he would fight again and added that he believed he had disgraced himself. Next came Liston, wearing a blue shirt, blue slacks, and a white straw hat.

"When I heard the crowd boo me, I said to myself that I would fix them. And now if the public doesn't like me, they're just going to have to live with it until they can find someone who can beat me."

Nobody asked him about Cassius Marcellus Clay.

Everything went downhill after that. Liston would be humiliated twice by Clay, who would soon after change his name to Muhammad Ali. After their second fight—which featured a bizarre who-saw-the-punch knockout and concluded with the crowd chanting, "Fix . . . fix . . . fix"—Liston became a pariah hammered with scorn and ridicule all across the continental land mass. He was near broke and near friendless, but he did not go quietly into the limbo of oblivion.

Instead, he went to Las Vegas. And why not? He needed a home where a man's place on past police blotters would not be held against him. Wasn't it Bugsy Siegel who irrigated (with mob money) that slice of land under the neon sun, which then morphed into the Las Vegas Strip? Wasn't it the same mob that regained control of its investment by murdering him? And wasn't one of the top suspects in that ambush Frankie Carbo?

Admittedly, things were changing in Vegas, but Liston wasn't the first fallen celebrity to seek asylum in the land of the green felt jungle. It was not surprising that the town's upper echelon of society didn't rush to welcome him. For most of his life, champion or not, Liston had always been on the outside looking in.

Perhaps the person in his new hometown that he felt closest to and trusted the most was Johnny Tocco, who had known him back in St. Louis where Tocco ran an old school boxing gym around the time Liston turned pro. Tocco moved his operation to Las Vegas in 1953 and set up shop at the edge of downtown Vegas at the corner of Charleston and Main.

The joint was a reflection of Tocco's no-nonsense approach to his pupils. It was small, and under the Vegas sun it was broiling hot. Ron Kantowski, a local sports columnist of serious stature, once told me that the aroma of Tocco's gym reminded him of a blend of soiled, sweaty socks mingled with the smell of very old and overused protective cups.

In short, Liston was comfortable there. It was a reflection of the life he had known since his first fight in the amateurs, and Tocco genuinely cared about him. It was a place where he felt safe because, as Tocco would say, "Practically every fighter from a big city learned how to box in a gym like this. They feel at home here." Liston was no exception.

With Tocco's encouragement, Liston would launch what he believed could be a serious comeback beginning July 1, 1966—thirteen cities and a trip to Mexico, sixteen wins and fifteen knockouts.

But only one rated fighter was on the list: Leotis Martin, Liston's old sparring partner from the Philadelphia gyms. Martin knocked Liston out in the ninth round with a single punch at the old International Hotel and Casino, soon to become the Las Vegas Hilton.

Nobody paid much attention to that result except Liston. His record at that point was 49–4 with thirty-nine knockouts and, with one more bout left on the tour, he was determined to make that last fight a showpiece. After all, he was still a ranked fighter. It was a showcase that never happened.

His last stand on the trip came on June 29, 1970, at the old Jersey City Armory, an outdated building reminiscent of an abandoned aircraft hangar. The opponent was Chuck Wepner, the pride and hometown hero of nearby Bayonne, New Jersey, and on whom the Rocky movies were based. Wepner's fans packed the joint.

It was no contest. Liston sliced and decked Wepner's face early and dropped him in the fifth with a thunderous body blow. Referee Barney Felix stopped the bout between the ninth and tenth rounds. Wepner, always a profuse bleeder, needed seventy-two stitches to repair the damage. The only memorable thing to come out of it was Liston's locker room quote afterward. A sportswriter asked Liston if Wepner was the bravest man he ever saw. Thinking about it, Liston replied, "No, his manager be."

There were no big purses for Liston's last tour. It was far more a treadmill run than a return to prominence. Liston returned to Vegas, both his income and his self-esteem seriously damaged.

Liston desperately needed money. Toward that end, they proposed a fight against George Chuvalo in the Montreal Forum. Six months after the Chuck Wepner fight, the day Chuvalo wired the promoter to accept the terms, newspapers were found piling up at Liston's front door. Liston's car was in the driveway, and inside the house the undiscovered dead body of Sonny Liston lay sprawled across his bed. He had been dead for almost a week.

In death, Charles Sonny Liston was even more of an enigma than he had been alive. What we know about the circumstances surrounding his death leads to far more questions than answers. This is what we know for certain.

In late December 1970, Geraldine Liston had taken their two children back to St. Louis for a two-week visit with relatives. On January 4 or 5, Geraldine called Tocco and told him she had not heard from Liston in three days. He called the police, who broke in.

Tocco later told a friend, "The living room furniture was in disarray. Liston was on the bed with a needle sticking out of his arm." However, Dennis Caputo, one of the police interviewed for the documentary *Sonny Liston: The Champ Nobody Wanted*, said he found no syringes or needles, just a quarter ounce of heroin in a balloon in the kitchen and a half ounce of marijuana in Liston's pants pocket. However, there was no spoon to cook the heroin or a tourniquet to help inject it. Former Las Vegas police detective Gary Beckwith said, "It was not uncommon in these cases for families to go through and tidy up to save the family embarrassment."

The Las Vegas Police called it death due to overdose. But the coroner, Mark Herman, said he believed the body had been undiscovered for about six days, which meant it was too decomposed to run toxicology tests. He, therefore, ruled it death through lung congestion and heart failure. Liston had been hospitalized a month earlier for chest pains.

Was it a tragic overdose of heroin or was it a "hot shot"? Did Liston miscalculate and administer a deadly dose, or did somebody else do it to him? There was no shortage of theories, some of them off the wall and others not so outside the realm of possibility. The first theory states that Liston had been involved as a collector for Vegas loan sharks. He tried to extort money from them in return for his silence, and they did him in. According to the second theory, Liston always bought drugs at a house on the west side of town. One day, as usual, he had gone there to make a buy, and, coincidentally, the cops arrived shortly after for a bust. Because Liston had ratted on them, theorists say, they killed him. Finally, a third theory suggests that Liston had been instructed to throw the Wepner fight on that final tour but had double crossed the alleged fixers just before the fight. The angry fixers who had lost money then murdered him.

One name repeatedly connected to Liston's death through rumor was that of Ash Resnick, a "connected" figure on the strip. He first came out to Vegas as the "athletic director" for The Thunderbird Hotel. Since this was not the Catskills Borscht Belt, one had to wonder what his title meant. He was also at Caesars Palace, the Aladdin, the Dunes, the Tropicana, the old El Rancho, and Maxim hotel. In 1974, Resnick was convicted of income tax evasion while employed at Caesars Palace. The government alleged that Resnick skimmed more than three hundred thousand dollars from Caesars and failed to pay taxes on it. The decision was later overturned. Resnick was very close with the mob, and he was close with Liston. At one point, he was said to have hired Liston as a bodyguard.

Beyond rumors, he was never connected to Liston's death. However, he was named in an FBI report regarding the first Liston–Ali fight, in which he is quoted as telling an associate, Barnett Magids, to bet heavy on Liston. He then reverses his stand in a subsequent telephone call, emphatically saying, "Don't bet anything. I'll explain later." The twin caveats here are, first, that the FBI never proved anything and, second, knowing the paranoia and proclivities of FBI Director Herbert Hoover, agents often substituted the wish for the deed in memos sent directly to please Hoover.

With this last in mind, local police accepted suicide as the cause and closed the case. The passage of decades has only embellished what has become a legend.

It is mid-February of 2015 in Las Vegas. Beyond the neon glitz and garish architecture of the Strip, this is a desert-scaped town, except for the myriad of parks and baseball fields—and the cemeteries.

The morning traffic along Eastern Avenue is never casual. People go to work. People go to shop. People are in a Las Vegas hurry. After the right turn into Davis Memorial Park, the stark hum of traffic seems to melt against the song of birds from the trees overlooking the sudden serenity.

A black stone marker just inside the entrance bears the legend, GARDEN OF PEACE. "Use the big fountain as a landmark," we had been told at the office, "then walk parallel to it. You'll find his grave not far from where a number of children are buried." Actually, it was a little closer than that, next to a plaque that bears the words, margaret m cassidy, AGE 71.

This is the final resting place of Charles Sonny Liston. The memorial marker simply says, CHARLES SONNY LISTON, and beneath it just two words, A MAN.

He has no relatives and few friends still left in Las Vegas. And yet, we are not the only recent visitors to this gravesite. In the middle of the nameplaque, four loose pennies form a strange corporal's guard. There was a time when pennies on a dead man's eyelids were meant as payment for the ferryman at the River Styx. In the wake of World War II, coins on a grave were also proof to a fallen comrade that a friend had visited the grave and given an advance payment so the departed could pay for drinks when they got together again.

There are those four coins and a sprig of red artificial flowers.

Who put these markers there and why? The cemetery staff had no answers.

THREE

And a Man-Child Shall Lead Them

"Yond Cassius has a lean and hungry look,
He thinks too much; such men are dangerous."
—*Julius Caesar, Julius Caesar, Act I, Scene 2*

"If I say a mosquito can pull a plough don't argue,
just hitch him up."
—*Muhammad Ali*

We were in Rome for the 1960 Olympics. As far as the United States' main priority was concerned, these were the games of sprinter Wilma Rudolph, long jumper Ralph Boston, pole vaulter Don Bragg, and a basketball team led by Oscar Robertson and Jerry West.

When it came to boxing, the Olympic light heavyweight division was about as relevant to fans back home as a father-son sack race at an Elks club Fourth of July picnic. In this country, Olympic boxing is all about the heavyweights. Moreover, the Poles had a multiple medal–winner named Zbigniew Pietrzykowski, who was the tournament's heavy favorite. Against him, the US sent an inexperienced eighteen-year-old named Cassius Marcellus Clay.

For the first two rounds, the experts were right. Clay was told just before the third, and final, round that he probably needed a knockout to win. He didn't get one, but he hit the Pole with an incredible flurry from the bell right up to the finish, winning the fight. For the next few days, with the medal draped around his neck, he buttonholed anyone who would stop in the Olympic Village to proclaim who he was and what he had done.

Thus did Cassius Clay cross the Rubicon that divides ordinary Americans from the dizzying heights of celebrity. Back in Louisville, he realized that what he had achieved was flattering but without economic reward. The clock was now ticking on his ability to cash in on the heroics of Rome. Toward that end, he sought out the late Bill King, an honest fight promoter who had also brought harness racing to the area. In the late 1980s, I sat with King in his office at Louisville Downs to talk about Clay's professional debut.

"He had just gotten home from the Olympics, and he came to see me," King recalled. "His exact words were, 'I got my medal, Mr. King, and now I want to turn pro. It's time for me to make some money.'"

The scramble to manage him involved a lot of folks, mainly Bill Martin, a local cop who was his trainer in the amateurs; Bill Reynolds, who was a local and an heir to the Reynolds aluminum money; and Bill Faversham, who put together a consortium of local moneyed people he called the Louisville Sponsoring Group. With all that prestige and economic muscle, the Faversham group won. For the first fight, he would be managed by a man who owned the local African American newspaper and trained by a guy named Stoner. Both were black.

"It must have been a delicate chore at that point," I said.

"Very, very difficult." King said. "He was in so many ways still very much an amateur. This is a good sports town, so we had a lot of folks here who knew he had won the gold. On top of that, we had a very interested black population rooting for him. We had to make sure not to have the thing blow up before it got rolling.

"I wanted a white guy who couldn't punch. I had to go all the way to Fayetteville, West Virginia, to find him. His name was Tunney Hunsaker. We made the fight, and they came. We had a really good crowd at Freedom Hall over in the Fair Grounds. Cassius won easily, but none of us thought he looked very good. Actually, it was a very dull fight. What helped create the identity that we wanted was having him wear his Olympic trunks with the words *USA* on the side. We paid him two thousand dollars. I never paid a first-time pro that much money before or since."

The Faversham group agreed with King. Even with their limited boxing knowledge, they knew that for their plans to come to fruition, it was time to get down to serious business. It was Bill Faversham who made the decision to send Clay down to Miami Beach, where Angelo Dundee had a stable of fighters in the 5th Street Gym. Angelo was a veteran trainer who had learned the trade first-hand as a kid from a veteran of the New York gyms, Chickie Ferrara. The decision was arrived at only after a lot of deliberation. Angelo's brother, Chris, a promoter in the Miami area, seemed to pose a problem to Faversham because his name had been mentioned in the Kefauver hearings. But after some soul searching and a study of Angelo's track record, they told Clay he was headed for Miami Beach.

The world Clay stepped into was a well-trafficked area just a few blocks long at the very edge of a downtown shopping district in Miami Beach. The focal point, at the corner of Fifth and Collins Avenue, was the 5th Street Gym, a second-floor walkup owned by Chris Dundee. The first floor belonged to a Walgreens drug store.

Across the street was a pawn shop. It was there, local legend goes, that Jake LaMotta pawned his middleweight championship belt after first prying the jewels out. Further up Collins Avenue was a luncheonette where Dundee's fighters who lived nearby, such as Clay, ate their meals. Eight doors down was a rooming house where Clay and a sparring partner shared a small room with a single bed. It was hardly a suitable setting for a king in waiting. On the other hand, it was a neighborhood devoid of distractions, where Clay took the first tentative steps of his education as a professional boxer.

Two months after his debut in Louisville, he began to fight in Miami Beach. He ran off a string of four straight knockouts, the fourth against a fair journeyman fighter named Donnie Fleeman, who had a 35–11–1 record. That set the stage for his triumphant return to Louisville. Bill King put him back into Freedom Hall against a twenty-eight-year-old Utah chicken farmer named LaMar Clark who, by fighting mostly guys with the skills of unemployed shepherds, had amassed a record of forty-four straight knockouts. Clark had gained national prominence by fighting six opponents (with questionable credentials) and knocking out all of them on the same night.

Off this last bit of fame, on April 19, 1961, an audience packed Freedom Hall. It was Clay's first serious moment as a pro. He dominated Clark, knocking him out in the second round. He was ready for prime time. They took the show to Las Vegas, where Clay won by unanimous decision over Duke Sabedong, then wound up winning three more fights. On February 10, 1962, he ran into Sonny Banks, a heavyweight contender managed by a labor leader named Big Julie Isaacson.

Isaacson was a friend of mine and a colorful character. That night, Isaacson came within an eyelash of getting banned for life. Banks knocked Clay down in the first round—the first knockdown for him as a pro. Clay returned the favor in the second. Then a funny thing happened to Clay on his way to a victory before the national media in New York City.

A slight trickle of blood became visible over Banks's eye. Referee Ruby Goldstein immediately threw his arms around Banks and waved an end to the fight. Seconds later, Isaacson tried to put his own hands around Goldstein, with very bad intentions. It took the intervention of three special cops to rescue the referee. Isaacson, shouting all the while about the "matchmaker protecting Clay," was finally hauled out of the ring.

Seven fights later, at a fight I covered, Clay got the biggest gift of his career. On March 13, 1963, he was matched in the Garden against an over-stuffed light heavyweight named Doug Jones. It almost derailed the date they were planning for him to take on the heavyweight champion, Sonny Liston. The judges that night, Frank Forbes and Artie Aidala, had the fight at 5–4–1 and the referee, who voted in those days, had it at an incredible 8–1–1. The sophisticated New York boxing audience damn near set a decibel record as the boos poured down from every corner of the building. Against that backdrop, it was clear that Clay needed a dramatic victory to set up a Liston fight. To get it, they shipped him off to London.

Henry Cooper, later knighted by the Queen, was an accomplished boxer with a ferocious left hand. What God had also given him, unfortunately, was a set of incredibly high cheekbones with thin skin to match. A punch off Cooper's face was always the key to opening the Red Sea.

In Wembley Stadium before a packed house on June 18, 1963, Henry Cooper brought the hometown fans one of the biggest thrills in British heavyweight history. He knocked Clay down with a punishing left hook, one so severe he had to be assisted back to his corner on quivering legs when round four ended. A lot of ringsiders were convinced he would not answer the bell for round five. What happened next still remains a matter of conjecture. There was a tear in one of Clay's gloves, and a replacement was needed. Some say Angelo helped make the tear bigger, some say he didn't have anything to do with it. There was a short delay, and British fans insisted it gave Clay time to recover. He stopped Cooper a round later on multiple cuts.

It was hard to believe. The wild ride was over. Clay's bad poems ("He wants to mix, so he'll go in six"), the photo opportunities with Hollywood stars, the late-night television appearances on all three major channels—the greatest campaign ever waged by an athlete to make himself an American household name—had created a celebrity in the age of television.

Now the biggest step of all was next, one which even his army of admirers really doubted he could pull off. He was set to fight the toughest champion since Rocky Marciano. Sonny Liston was a bully who could turn an opponent's legs to jelly with nothing more than his angry stare. It would come down to Liston and Clay in Miami Beach. It was preceded a month earlier by the first mass electronic pre-fight boxing press conference in history.

Out in Vegas, the books, opening line made Clay a 6–1 underdog. When told the news at the press conference, he trumpeted, "I am getting louder every day. I float like a butterfly, I sting like a bee. I am shocked by the odds. They make me a poor man's dream. By the way, Mr. Director, which camera am I on?"

Mercifully, the remote camera brought up Sonny Liston in Florida. Did he really dislike Clay? "You got kids at home?" Liston asked. "You know, if a kid don't mind you, he got to be put in his place. You got to give him a real good spanking. He shouldn't talk that way, but I want to thank him. He did what nobody else could do. He made me popular."

But, of course, young Clay would never even think of conceding the last word, so the screen shifted back to Miami, and Clay waved his finger, shouting, "He once was the villain, but there's a new villain in town. I am the villain. Make sure you get your villains straight. Put your money on me." Then the screen dumped to black.

Meanwhile, down in Miami, much to co-promoters Bill McDonald and Chris Dundee's horror, the fight was laying a massive dinosaur egg. Most of South Florida thought Clay was a great salesman but not so much a fighter. As if that wasn't bad enough, the box office had yet another worry. There were serious rumors that Cassius Clay had been thinking of joining the Nation of Islam, colloquially called the Black Muslims. It was a religious group led by Elijah Muhammad, dedicated to a version of Islam that demanded separation of blacks from whites. Unbeknownst to the rest of the public, Clay, soon to become Muhammad Ali, had already converted.

Malcolm X, who at the time was a spokesman for the Nation, showed up in Miami. He was charismatic and very visible, and local newspapers carried news of his arrival. Bill McDonald, who was drowning in a sea of red ink, met with him at the Hampton House Motel and Villas, the only black-owned hotel in Miami at the time, and proposed he leave and come back for the fight with a ringside ticket provided by McDonald. Malcom agreed, but it still didn't help ticket sales. The bottom line was that nobody believed in Cassius Clay. On fight night, the arena would be an acre of empty seats.

The morning of the fight, it seemed more a comedy of errors than ever. Clay was on time for the weigh-in, and so was Liston. What wasn't on time was the scale. They had to sit around for half an hour, waiting for it to arrive. Heavyweight weigh-ins are almost always an empty ritual. There is no weight to make in order to fight as a heavyweight. However, what happened there gave new meaning to the definition of chaos. It began not with a whimper but with the loudest bang South Florida had ever heard.

The doors of the Miami Beach Convention Center were thrown open, and the decibel level of that bang was positively dwarfed by what followed. The man-child of all boxing on the planet came bellowing through the empty hall and toward the stage, with a sound matched only by the roar of the 20th Century Limited passenger train.

"Where is he? Where is that big, ugly bear? Get him out here. Get him out here now. We can get the fight over with right now. Come on and take your whupping, Bear." As he shouted, he punctuated each individual word by slamming the point of the African walking sick in his hand against the floor. Each staccato clatter rocked the confusion into a riotous chaos.

He shouted, he stomped, he challenged. With each insult he moved closer and closer to Liston. The fighters' blood pressures were taken and the doctor, Alexander Robbins, shook his head back and forth. "Clay's pressure is in the stroke area. His pulse has jumped by forty-five beats per minute. He is scared to death. He is using up his energy at a frightening rate."

When they weighed in, Clay was still talking. He never stopped talking. Almost forgotten in the confusion was the fact that Clay was both heavier and taller than the most feared heavyweight in the world.

The only words I can recall from Liston were a surprisingly soft, "Shut up." A blessed silence took possession of the room. I remember thinking, *Well, maybe he ain't so dumb.* Then I thought, *No, maybe he has just lost his mind.*

Later that afternoon as I was driving up Collins Avenue, I flipped on the car radio in time to hear, "Reliable sources report that the challenger was seen two hours after the weigh-in purchasing a plane ticket at the airport. As far as we know at this point, the fight is still on." In fact, Clay was back at his hotel, sound asleep.

Over the seven decades in which I have covered sports in general, and boxing in particular, I can't recall a day like that one.

It was the evening of February 25, 1964. It did not take anyone long to realize that this was not going to be a night like all other nights. In the first fight of the evening, Clay's younger brother,

Rudolph Valentino Clay, made his professional boxing debut. In truth, for Rudolph, that night was a kind of hey-buddy-don't-give-up-the-day-job experience (although he won). He was not very good, but the other guy was worse. During the fight, I heard a voice yelling as though the speaker were sitting right on my lap. In fact, it was coming from an aisle twenty feet away where Cassius Marcellus Clay was shouting instructions to Rudolph, who was in a four-rounder. Clay wore an open-throated t-shirt and dark slacks. He bore no resemblance to the wild man who had confronted Liston at the weigh-in.

This was the guy whose blood pressure was supposed to be in the stroke range that morning. This was the guy who had been seen buying a plane ticket out of town later that afternoon. As he often said in our relationship that followed, "Fooled ya."

As the biblical saying goes, "Out of the mouths of babes comes gems of the truth." What followed next was reason enough to call this National Children's Night. From the very beginning of the fight, it was hard to believe our eyes. Clay came out dancing, circled counterclockwise even as the tassels on his white boxing shoes did a dance of their own, and smacked Liston in the mouth with a jab. He danced, he wriggled, and he leaned back to avoid getting hit—an amateurish move he surely should not have done. However, in Clay's case, all it did was easily win him the opening round. Liston was short with his punches. He was embarrassed. He was angry. The crowd was absolutely stunned.

Two rounds or six minutes later, Clay bounced a right hand off the area under Liston's eye, and blood began to flow on the face of Mount Rushmore. Clay threw punches in bunches and shouted at Liston with each punch. For the first time, at least in my memory, Sonny Liston backed up.

Then a strange thing happened. After round four, there was a commotion in Clay's corner. From my seat across the ring, I could see two guys I recognized as members of The Nation who were in

Clay's corner, arguing with Dundee while he rubbed a towel across Clay's face and then rubbed it across his own. Clay was shouting that he could not see. Nobody had a clue what was happening except, perhaps, Liston's corner.

Earlier, a coagulant had been used to stop the blood from streaming down Liston's face just below one eye. From the rapidity with which the skin under the eye turned black, I suspected it might have been monsel, a substance outlawed because of its danger to the eyes but still very much in use back then. Either by accident or design, it had gotten onto Liston's gloves, and some of it may have gotten into Clay's eyes.

Clay did the only thing he could do in round five. He ran like a thief and occasionally got hit like a catcher's mitt. But by round six his vision had cleared, and he was back in charge. Liston looked terrible, and he was positively mauled. This was how Sonny Liston relinquished the championship that night: not on his shield, but sitting head down in his corner and not moving when the bell chimed for round seven. He did not get up. He had surrendered. The Bear had been caged.

Clay spent the night at the Hampshire House Motel and Villas where Malcom X had checked back in. It was there that he celebrated the most important night of his twenty-two-year-old life.

It was the start of the Clay-who-became-Ali era. Like almost everything we've known about Ali for decades, it started with a shock. In those days, it was traditional for all heavyweight championship fights to be followed by a press conference the next day.

Clay went beyond anyone's expectations. For starters, he told us he was no longer Cassius Clay. He was now Cassius X until Elijah Muhammad, in his words, "got rid of my slave name and gave me my real one." When asked if he was to now be active in the civil rights movement, his answer was a real stunner.

"I'm a citizen everywhere in the world; I am a citizen. I don't need civil rights. I am supposed to have them . . . I do not want integration. I look in the jungle, and I see the tigers with the tigers . . . black ants with black ants. I want to be with my own. What happens to people who try to integrate? They put dogs on them. Nine out of ten whites think that way. I don't want that . . . I'm free. I don't have to be what you want me to be."

As always, he was sincere in what he believed, as sincere as I found him when we later discussed why he would not go into the army, as sincere as when he eventually left the Nation of Islam to become an orthodox Sunni Muslim.

He would soon become Muhammad Ali. Whatever you think of that, you have to concede one thing—you could never call him boring.

There was still unfinished business. The Nilons were invoking the contractual rematch clause, and Ali and Liston were supposed to meet again in Boston. Liston went to Plymouth Rock, where he trained as never before. He was in the best shape of his career, the kind of shape he would need to beat Ali. But three nights before the scheduled fight, all hell broke loose. Ali was in terrific pain; he had developed a strangulated hernia.

The fight was postponed for six months. We didn't know it at the time, but Liston's age precluded him from ever getting back into the shape he had worked to achieve at Plymouth Rock. Moreover, his prior mob associations came back to haunt the entire production. The Suffolk County District Attorney Garrett Byrne objected to Sam Silverman, the local promoter in Boston, who was alleged to have mob ties. The promotion was tied up in court. Finally, Intercontinental Promotions, Inc., a firm organized to promote Liston's fights, tired of the delay and pulled out. The fight was moved to Lewiston, Maine, a mill town of forty-one thousand residents and home of the Bates Bedspread Factory.

What history should remember as Muhammad's Wonderful Adventure began with a bus trip. From the champ's camp in Chicopee, Massachusetts, we drove 120 miles north. It was yet another showcase for Ali. As the last writer boarded the bus, Ali announced,

"Don't worry about the trip. If we get into trouble, I'll do something religious. I'll take up a collection."

When we arrived at the Holiday Inn in Auburn, Maine, four hours later, about 150 people were lined up to see the champ. In Auburn, that's a sizable gathering. A local reporter asked Ali what he thought so far of the people in Maine. "I don't know," he replied. "They all look alike to me."

It was May 23, 1965, two days before fight night in Lewiston, and the home away from home for Inter continental Productions (ICP) had all the charm of a buggy-whip manufacturing plant the day it lapsed into bankruptcy. Nestled cozily between the Bill Davis Smoke Shop and the Rendezvous Bar, the ICP office was staffed by eight bored employees waiting for something—anything at all—to happen. The excitement became boundless when a lone pedestrian walked through the door and asked to see a seating chart. (He left without buying a ticket.)

Business proceeded at this same frenetic pace the rest of the day. It became apparent that this could be the only championship fight— hell, maybe the only fight, *period*—where the media and freeloaders outnumbered the paying customers.

Next door at the Bill Davis Smoke Shop, a lady, claiming to be a lifelong fight fan, was leaving just as I entered in time to hear her say, "Don't forget to notify me when they cut the price on the $25 tickets, Bill." Clearly, Lewiston was not going to be awed by its ten-day stint as the fight capital of the world. It vowed, however, to protect both fighters from a danger either real or hallucinatory, depending on with whom you spoke. There were rumblings that Ali in particular was in danger because the growing blood feud between Malcolm X and Elijah had resulted in the former's assassination. I had read in the paper that morning that three hundred police were expected to be on hand. "That's gotta be thirty police," a sport at the Smoke Shop told me. "Ain't three hundred police in the whole state of Maine."

That morning, I was having coffee with Angelo Dundee in the Auburn Holiday Inn, and I happened to look through the window behind us. There was Ali, a lone figure in a sweat suit, running through the hills—no guards . . . no cops . . . no retinue. I said to Dundee, "Some threat, some bullshit."

At 7:30 p.m. on fight night, Lewiston was ready for the main event—not inside but outside of St. Dom's high school's hockey arena. The small cavalcade of cars inched down Lisbon Street and made the turn onto Birch. At every corner, people with kids and ice cream watched the self-proclaimed fight crowd drive by. Some of them waved and cheered. It was more fun, the locals agreed, than a clam bake.

At precisely 10:15 p.m., with eight current and former world champions assembled in the ring and Robert Goulet struggling to remember the words as he sang our National Anthem, Sonny Liston began the trek toward ringside. The hard guy stare had evaporated under the intense heat generated by the television lights. He was greeted with a roar. There was much to be said about what Liston had become. His opponent was the only fighter in the world capable of making him a sentimental favorite. And he was the only fighter in the world capable of declining the privilege. Then, almost with rub of a magic lamp, Muhammad Ali was facing him in the center of the ring, awaiting instructions from the referee, Joe Walcott. It was the evening's last sense of law and order. Unkind people also say it was the last moment Walcott had anything to do with the fighters.

Liston fought with the nimble grace of a web-footed butcher auditioning for the Bolshoi Ballet. He fought just as he had done back in Miami Beach during act one of this morality play, which is to say he charged, huffed, and puffed, but couldn't lay a glove on the champion.

Without warning, what followed was the perfect punch, or the result of mass hallucination, or a swan dive worthy of Olympic competition. This much I do know, despite the fierce opposition to my belief. I've watched those film replays over and over. Liston charged and missed, charged and missed, and charged and missed, ad infinitum. Ali's right hand was cocked high, and on one of those lunges where Liston was totally off balance, Ali chopped straight down with his right hand, more of a push than punch. I believe he did indeed make contact. It was not the Hammer of Thor, but rather more like tag in the playground where "you're it." Liston was so far off balance he had nowhere to go but down—and that qualifies as a punch.

Ali stood over him, screaming, "Get up, sucker. Get up. Nobody will believe this," until Walcott forcibly shoved him toward a neutral corner before returning to the scene of the crime. Liston was in the same position in which Walcott had last seen him. Ali was still yelling in rage. Was it enough to keep a five-year-old kindergartner down? Hell, no. However, with Ali shrieking and the crowd choking in amazement, Liston chose to stay down.

Walcott wobbled around in circles, searching for the knockdown timekeeper to pick up the count. Liston, supine, looked for Walcott. Ali looked across the ring at Liston. As Walcott continued to look for the timekeeper, with his back turned to the fighters, they simply got up, unsure of what to do, and began to fight again. Oblivious, Walcott caught the eye of a diminutive man at ringside who was standing on his chair, screaming at him. The man was Nat Fleischer, editor of *The Ring Magazine*. Measured against the heavyweight fighters, he looked like a Lilliputian, with a bow tie to match and very little hair. However, in the boxing business, Fleischer was a man of huge influence. With Walcott's attention on him, Fleischer drew a finger across his neck as he yelled, "Eight . . . nine . . . ten." Walcott got the idea and ended the fight after the longest long count in history. The instant he did, a full-throated chant from the fifty-dollar seats echoed through the arena, over and over: "Fix . . . fix . . . fix." The audience had paid to see a title fight, but all they got was a mystery that took fewer than three minutes to play out.

Back in the dressing room, Liston, wearing a white t-shirt, jeans, and a green zippered jacket, kept repeating: "I was trying to hear the count." Him and everyone else in the joint.

Indirectly, the night was boxing's answer to criticism about the sport's brutality. A pacifist like Mahatma Gandhi could have refereed this one and been on familiar ground.

Later that night at a post-fight victory party—the one the champion did not attend—the Louisville Sponsoring Group, the Nation of Islam, and the few remaining fight people mingled in search of answers. The fight mob, which didn't own the title anymore; the LSG country club set, which thought it did; and the Nation of Islam, to which the champion was pledged, all tried to figure out what had happened.

"Angelo," the wife of one of them pleaded, "what happened? What will people say?"

"What happened was that our man hit him, he went down, and he did not get up. What happened was when you don't get up, the fight is over."

"What will the writers say?"

"Go ask them."

A couple came up to me. "We're Mr. and Mrs. Cutchins from Louisville. What are you going to write about this?"

"Funny you should ask," I said. "I'm still wondering about that."

Boxing survived, as it always does. So did Lewiston, as illustrated the next morning by the cab driver who took several of us to the airport. He drove in silence while my companion took apart everything about the state, the town, and the countryside. When he turned into a dirt road, my companion said, "Beautiful, do we have to stop and milk the cows?"

"Well," the driver said, deadpan, "That would depend on what time it is."

Lewiston took care of itself in that instant far better than Liston did.

Five months later, Ali's red World Champion bus lumbered upstate to Catskill, New York, where Floyd Patterson was training for their fight on November 22, 1965. After his workout, Patterson answered questions from the media and spectators, when suddenly the king of all hecklers yelled from the back of the room: "He can't fight. He runs. He's scared. I officially nickname him 'the Rabbit.' And when I fight him it won't be a boxing match. It will be a rabbit hunt."

To nobody's surprise, Ali stopped Patterson in the twelfth round.

Until his conversion to the Nation of Islam, combined with his refusal to be drafted in the military, turned the boxing industry into a constitutional battlefield, Ali fought seven more times and won them all. One of those bouts was of particular interest to me.

Ali was in Toronto to fight George Chuvalo, a courageous but totally over-matched hometown boxer. It came at a time when a lot of America's young men sought and were granted political asylum in Canada because they did not believe in the Vietnam War. It was the main reason I went to Toronto, fully knowing there was virtually no way Ali could lose. It was also the cause of our first and only argument when, three days before the fight, I found him in in an old, creaking, tired joint named Sully's Gym.

I walked into a desultory room dominated by a sagging ring and windows that looked as though they hadn't been washed since John L. Sullivan was champ in 1882. I walked past the *Gym Dues* and *No Spitting* signs until I saw Ali, facedown on a rubbing table while his masseur Luis Saria worked him over.

Ali propped himself up on an elbow.

"Hey, what are you doing here?"

"Somebody said there's going to be a fight," I replied.

"Aw, you know this ain't no fight."

Then I hit him with the question I had come to ask. Was he planning to join the swelling ranks of draft-dodgers and war objectors in Canada? I knew his answer before I asked the question, but I was stunned by the vehemence with which he expressed it.

He jumped off the table.

"I thought you knew me better than that. America is my home. Do you think I would let somebody chase me out of my home? Nobody is going to chase me out of my birthplace. If they say I have to go to jail, then I will. But I'm not gonna run away, and you should know it."

Ali won easily and went on to fight in England and Houston, Texas, twice, and once each in Germany and New York. It was in Houston that he had refused to take the oath at the draft board. And it was after the Zora Folley fight at Madison Square Garden (he won by technical knockout in the seventh) that the dramatic rift that divided America over Vietnam came to a head and crashed down on Ali.

The Louisville draft board had reclassified Muhammad as 1A after the government lowered the standards on the mental test. Ali appealed on the claim as a conscientious objector. The appeal was denied. What happened in between the appeal and the draft board's denial of it was not public knowledge. The process itself was two-pronged: an FBI report and an interview with a Department of Justice examiner named Lawrence Grauman. According to the United States Court of Appeals for the Fifth Circuit, No. 24,991, "the appellant [was] sincere in his objection on religious grounds to a participation in war of any form and recommended the conscientious objector claim of the registrant be sustained."

However, in one of the rare cases involving the Selective Service Act, a draft board overruled the Justice Department examiner. Ali was stripped of his title. He was denied licenses to fight in state after state, and in such cities as Seattle, New York, Detroit, Columbus, Tampa, and Miami; as well as a host of other places, such as an Indian reservation in Arizona. Additionally, when he was offered bouts in London and Toronto, the State Department and the Justice Department interfered. Ali had not fought since March 22, 1967. He was a champion without a title, a fighter deprived of a way to make a living. All of this started when he had yet to be indicted and continued during his appeal.

Meanwhile, the divided passions over both the Vietnam War and Ali himself grew more intense each day. A large segment of America's sportswriters and columnists bordered on the vitriolic in their harangues. Edwin Dooley, chairman of the New York State Athletic Commission, had denied Ali a license because of "actions detrimental to boxing." He and I debated this point over radio station WMCA on the Barry Gray Show, where I reminded him that he had approved the manager and trainer license of a known associate of Frankie Carbo.

"Well, I did because the fighter requested it and he wouldn't have been comfortable without him."

"What if he had requested Martin Bormann?" I asked.

Ann Wagner, one of Ali's lawyers, was granted a legal search of the commission's files by the court. She reported other cases of drugs, rape, and forgery where other fighters' licenses had been renewed. Meanwhile, a Georgia State Senator, Leroy Johnson, discovered that Georgia had no athletic commission. At Johnson's insistence, the City of Atlanta quickly enacted enabling legislation for a municipal boxing commission. This was on the heels of Governor of Georgia Lester Maddox's reversal, who had first said Ali could fight there and who later reversed his stance.

During this period, James Earl Jones was starring on Broadway in Howard Sackler's moving play *The Great White Hope*. It dealt with the eventual imprisonment of Jack Johnson, the first African American heavyweight champion, who, for lack of a better word, was framed because of a love affair with a white woman. The parallel with the injustice done to Ali struck me as incredible, particularly as I sat in the theater and heard Jones's booming voice fill the theater as he said, "Champ don't mean piss-all to me. Ah been it. All dat champ jive bin beat clear outta me. Dat belt of yours juss hardware, don't even 'ole my pants up. But Ahm stuck widdit, see, dis hunk of junky hardware that don't let go. It turnin' green on me, and it still ain't lettin' go. Ahm stuck widdit juss as y'all stuck tryna get it back from me."

With that quote still ringing in my ears, I went down to interview the governor, Lester Maddox, on June 26, 1970, who had at first welcomed the fight. When he suddenly realized what it would symbolize to the sizeable redneck portion of his base constituency, he banned it for political reasons. I believed the decision had been totally self-serving, and what he told me twenty seconds into the interview rubber-stamped that thought. He said with great passion, "It's a sad and tragic day when a man who will not fight for his country will get in the ring and fight for dollars. I have, therefore, proclaimed tomorrow night a night of mourning." Later that day, a local sports editor named Jesse Outlar told me, "If Lester wants to mourn, let him go mourn. The rest of us are going to the fight."

After two years and nine months in exile, Muhammad Ali walked into an unknowable future where he and nobody else had the slightest idea whether he could recapture the magic he once had. One thing was certain: down in Philadelphia there was a barrel-chested left hooker waiting to find out. His name was Joe Frazier.

FOUR

The Man Who Wasn't Ali

"You were there. You saw the fight. You know I won. So what
I got to do to convince everyone? What the hell I got to do?"

—*Joe Frazier, after Ali–Frazier I*

It was a moment that history ignored but that anyone who was
there to witness it has never forgotten. On an April day in 1971,
an African American man stood at the speaker's rostrum in the South
Carolina General Assembly. He was the first black man invited to
address that governmental body since the post–Civil War days of
Reconstruction.

His name was Joe Frazier, and a month earlier he had won the
heavyweight championship of the world by defeating Muhammad
Ali. Now, he was coming home to address the legislature in the state
where he was born—an invitation that, for many residents, was still
unthinkable seventeen years after the United States Supreme Court
had legally ended segregation of the races.

In the nerve center of a building over which a Confederate flag still flew, Joe Frazier looked over an audience that included three black legislators, the first few to win election since the Civil War. After noting that it was good to be home, Frazier smiled an enormous grin at the three and said, "I see there have been a few changes made around here since I left."

Then he told a story that indicated how significant those changes had been. To paraphrase, it went something like this.

In 1959, Frazier was fifteen years old and working as a day laborer on a farm owned by two brothers named Bellamy. "We didn't have much conversation between blacks and whites back then. Ours was pretty much like this.

"Me: 'Mornin', boss.'

"Boss: 'To the mule.'

"Me at noon: 'Lunch, Boss.'

"Boss: 'In an hour.'

"Me at twilight: 'Quittin' time, Boss.'

"Boss: 'In the morning.'"

Frazier drew a fair amount of laughter, and that was another change for this audience. He spoke about what it meant to him to be there and his hopes for what he called a new kind of unity, a new kind of conversation, and a new kind of coming together.

Seven months later, the folks who ran the South Carolina State Fair ended their own kind of segregation by abolishing "Negro Days." The echo of the words of a professional boxer may not have been the trigger for that, but who is to say that it wasn't?

In a real sense, Joe Frazier himself was an element of change. He was born into a milieu that all but dictated he could not possibly grow healthy enough, big enough, and strong enough to become the heavyweight champion of the planet.

When Frazier was sixteen and already gone from the South Carolina lowlands, a physician named Dr. Donald Garth outraged South Carolina's Beaufort County when he publicly announced the well-kept secret that too many of the county's underclass were dying because of malnutrition and diseases almost unheard of elsewhere in the country. It had been that way for decades. Garth treated cases of pellagra, a disease most of America thought was extinct. He spoke of a woman dying of a rampant infestation of maggots. He claimed 70 percent of the county's children five years old and younger had parasitic infections. Much of his constituency had no toilets or running water. That's the way it had always been, even on January 12, 1944, when Joe Frazier was born in a section of Beaufort called Laurel Bay, the twelfth child of Dolly and Rubin Frazier. His father was a one-armed farmer who barely etched a sharecropper's living out of the barren soil of his tiny acreage.

Ray Arcel, the great fight trainer, used to say, "Hard times can make monkeys eat red peppers." For the Fraziers, there was no shortage of that kind of struggle. Here was Rubin, the patriarch whose farm help consisted only of his kids. He was trying to scratch a living out of soil that the locals called "white dirt" because, according to the local blacks, it was the only kind of soil the power structure would let blacks have.

"With all the things Rubin had to do to make it when the land could only produce cotton and watermelons, he also had white lightning on the side [bootleg whiskey he made in a homemade still and sold to neighbors]," I said to Joe Frazier's son, Marvis. "How did he survive? How did he get the work done with only one arm? It's remarkable."

"Not really. He did whatever had to be done," Marvis replied. He laughed and added with the kind of conviction that would have made his dad smile, "No problem. My grandfather was a Frazier.

"One of my dad's jobs was to care for the pigs. They had one that was three hundred pounds, and daddy used a stick to get him to move. And the pig turned on him and chased him."

Joe, who was then around twelve years old, ran, tripped over a rock, and broke his left arm. There was no money for a doctor. The arm had to heal by itself and could no longer be extended anywhere near as far as the right arm. This may have been the reason Frazier had to work so much harder than most other fighters to develop strength in that arm.

It would become his most powerful weapon by far, giving him what had long been known in the gyms of Philly as a Philadelphia left hook—a misnomer in his case because of its genesis. What it was, was a Beaufort-inspired, hell-raising left hook.

When the arm healed, Joe had to help supplement the family income. He went to work on a farm owned by the Bellamy Brothers, and it was there that he saw one of the brothers beat an even younger farm employee savagely with a belt.

"You had to understand Beaufort County to know why he did what he did next," Marvis said. "It was Klan country, and the man warned Pop about what would happen if he ever told anyone what he had seen. Daddy took the little money he had and jumped on a bus for New York to live with my uncle Tommy."

But that didn't work so well. Tommy was married with children and had very little room in his apartment. Frazier felt he was putting the family out too much. He moved down the Jersey Turnpike to Philadelphia to live with his aunt, Evelyn. The city would make an impact on him every bit as much as Beaufort had.

Philly thought of itself as the boxing capital of America, and with good reason. The gyms of Philly made champions out of those who survived and destroyed those who didn't. Sparring sessions in these gyms too often degenerated into wars. As the late George Benton, one of the best Philly fighters of his era, once told me, "When I was in the gym back then, we had a hell of a lot of street fighters in boxing gloves who thought a sparring session meant they were fighting for the championship of the gym. A lot of careers were buried in this town just because of that."

Boxing had always fascinated Frazier, starting with the memory of those nights back in Beaufort when he and most of his siblings would crowd around a tiny black-and-white television set with their dad on Friday nights and watch boxing, generally from Madison Square Garden with Jimmy Powers doing the blow-by-blow. It was those fights that inspired him to stuff an old pillow case with a brick, rags, and moss, and mount it behind the house, punching it every day as though it were a heavy bag. He translated that wish to the deed by charging his young classmates to enlist him as a bodyguard of sorts to protect their lunch money from the older bullies. "I was damned good at that," he later said. He must have been, because it was at that age that one of his uncles began to call him "a little Joe Louis."

The impending marriage between Frazier and the boxing ring was inevitable, but it would have to wait. What he needed now was a job, and he found it in an improbable place in nearby Kensington on the killing floor of a kosher slaughterhouse, Cross Brothers, located at Front and Venango Streets. He split his time between the butchering floor and the cold floor where the split sides of beef were hung.

It was hard, brutal work on the killing floor and heavy duty lifting in the cold floor. In this latter floor, Joe Frazier surreptitiously drove his fists into the hanging beef carcasses as though they were heavy bags.

Sound familiar? It ought to if you saw the movie *Rocky*, written by and starring Sylvester Stallone. On more than one occasion, Joe said Stallone had a bunch of fighters who would come to Los Angeles to meet with him. "We went because we thought we might get in his movie. But he had us there just to pick our brains. He modeled his character after me, right down to my running up the steps of the Art Museum."

And then Frazier rediscovered boxing. The way Joe Hand, Sr., a retired Philadelphia police detective who later ran Joe's Cloverlay Gym, tells it, Frazier's intended purpose was to lose weight. "Joe had these enormous thighs," Hand explained. "He couldn't buy clothes without having them altered, and he didn't have the money for that.

So, at age seventeen, Frazier walked, unannounced, into the 23rd Street PAL Gym. The guy who ran it was a police sergeant named Duke Dugent. He explained to Frazier that it was a boxing gym and suggested he work out there with the rest of the guys to lose some weight.

"Now, it was a place where a lot of good fighters trained, and the way it was in Philly, places like the 23rd PAL, Champs down the street, and the Passyunk in South Philly were always active. Trainers would pick one closest to them and watch the fighters work. If a kid showed some potential, they would offer to train and even manage him.

"There was a guy named Yank Durham who hung out at the 23rd PAL just about every day after finishing his shift as a welder for the Pennsylvania Railroad. He took Joe under his wing."

Durham was a former boxer and World War II veteran. He knew the game well, and he was awfully good at first impressions. When Red Smith, a *New York Herald-Tribune* columnist, met him for the first time, he noted his deep voice and the way he was never at a loss for words, calling him the Everett Dirksen of managers.

Durham was a stern taskmaster in the gym who insisted on what he wanted. At some point, he had a very good heavyweight named Leotis Martin, a ferocious puncher who sometimes took time off during a fight. According to Joe Hand, Durham grew one thumbnail long and trimmed it into a point. "When Leotis came back after a slow round, Yank would reach in with one hand to remove the mouthpiece and stab him with the thumb on the other hand. Martin would yell, and Yank would tell him, "Hurts, don't it? It will hurt a hell of a lot more if you come back next round and that other son of a bitch is still standing." Martin must have been a good pupil because nineteen of his thirty-one victories came by knockout. As Frazier developed, Durham had the two spar. Because they fought so hard and Martin gave as much as he took, Durham never matched them in a real fight when both were under his control.

Frazier was improving, and Durham began to believe there was, indeed, a chemistry at work here. Starting in 1962, Frazier won the National Golden Glove heavyweight title three years in a row. Only a single loss to Buster Mathis marred his record over that period; Mathis was a deceptive opponent at 245 pounds because his foot speed made his weight a non-factor.

Frazier and Mathis were matched again in the trials for the 1964 Olympic Games scheduled for Tokyo. Both Durham and Duke Dugent, Frazier's first mentor at the 23rd Street PAL gym, were convinced that Mathis presented no problem. Both had without reservation committed their full faith and future plans to the pure power of the Frazier left hook.

But this was still an amateur fight, where the race is not always to be the strongest or the slickest. Often, the round went not to the harder or more effective puncher but rather to the one who ran away like a cat burglar in the night while jabbing semi-effectively. To compound Frazier's problem, body punchers like himself received almost no credit.

"All that fat boy did," Frazier said of his defeat by Mathis in the Olympic trials, "was to run like a thief, hit me with a peck, and then backpedal." Frazier's opponent also wore his trunks very high, and the amateur referee took two points away for low blows that really weren't. Mathis won the decision, and Frazier, despondent and angry, came home to Philly, about to pack it all in.

But the image of the left hook was still firmly planted in the backroads of the minds of his handlers. They cajoled, and they argued. They repeatedly let logic make their case and, in the end, finally convinced a reluctant Frazier to go to Tokyo as an alternate. Work hard, they said, and maybe—just maybe—fate would step in.

Fate did.

Frazier worked like Frazier, and Mathis worked like Mathis—which is to say, not very hard. The team's coaches were not overly disappointed when Mathis broke his thumb in a sparring session and Frazier became the designated American heavyweight. What few back home knew was that, as the tournament progressed, Frazier, ironically, had also broken his own thumb. But he never told anyone, and he eventually won the Olympic title.

Now it was time to make some money.

It was August 16, 1965, three months after Muhammad Ali stunned the world by stopping Sonny Liston a second time in Lewiston, Maine. Durham placed Frazier as a pro on the undercard of a Philadelphia fight card at Convention Hall, featuring a popular local super welterweight named Kitten Hayward. Frazier, who had brought Olympic gold back to Philly the year before, made his debut against a journeyman named Woody Goss. A left hook (what else?) dropped Goss in the first, and then, as Goss clutched and held repeatedly, the referee, Zack Clayton, stopped the bout with just 1:42 gone in that opening round.

Durham's advice to Frazier before that fight would morph into a regular pre-fight ritual, one that actually led to his nickname, Smokin' Joe Frazier: "All right, goddammit, I want you to go out and make smoke come from them gloves, understand?"

Frazier won the next four fights through a combination of Durham's cautious matchmaking and Frazier's thunderous left hook. Durham was an old-school trainer, schooled in the reality of the Philadelphia boxing rings. He had worked long and hard as a welder for the railroad. He had several good-to-very-good fighters, but he lacked the one thing necessary to steal a talented but young fighter to the championship: money.

Fortunately, a brilliant local lawyer named Bruce Wright soon brokered a marriage made in Philadelphia heaven. He introduced Durham and Frazier to the Reverend William Gray, a former college president and pastor at the prestigious Bright Hope Church on 12th Street. He and his son, William Gray III, a US congressman, then approached Dr. F. Bruce Baldwin, President of the Horn & Hardart

Baking Co—and the group Cloverlay (*clover* for luck and *overlay* for a bookie's term of a good bet) was born.

Entry price to Cloverlay was $250 a share. The mission statement was a weekly income for Frazier so he could leave the slaughterhouse and his part-time janitorial services at Bright Hope. The guaranteed share was 35 percent for Frazier and 15 percent for Durham. On the ownership roster were mostly the movers and shakers of Philly. And the underlying goal of Cloverlay was to give Durham the money needed to produce a champion.

Now there was money, and Durham was able to bring a new face into the mix, a Philadelphia cop, Joe Hand, Sr., who until then was living on a salary of just four thousand dollars a year. Hand read a story in the *Philadelphia Daily News* about the formation of the syndicate, borrowed five hundred dollars, and bought two shares. That five hundred dollars was worth twenty-eight thousand dollars by the time Frazier and Ali fought for the first time.

Hand's role soon became more than that of a shareholder. For a hundred dollars a month (which covered his monthly car loan note), he went to work for Bruce Wright as the office manager for Cloverlay. He ran the office, was a confidante of both Frazier and Durham, and wound up with the job of coming up with Frazier's own gym.

"The big thing," Hand told me, "was to get Joe out of the 23d Street PAL Gym and keep him out of places like Champ's—out of the gym wars of Philly. Durham wanted to orchestrate everything Joe did. This was Philadelphia boxing, and managers and trainers always worried about somebody trying to steal their fighter. Yank didn't want him dealing with reporters unless he was there to monitor the interview. He was obsessed with keeping the fighter isolated. That's how the Cloverlay Gym came into being.

"They sent me out to scout buildings and locations. We settled on North Philly because Joe was comfortable there and the North Philadelphia Station provided out-of-town writers easy access. I found an old factory that had become a dance hall at 2917

North Broad Street and Glenwood Avenue. I paid $87,000 for it and another $115,000 for the renovations. It was perfect for what Yank wanted.

"You had to be buzzed into the building, and Yank and I had the final say on everyone. There was a spectator section. We had a four-foot wall and a couple rows of chairs behind it. Nobody was ever allowed on the other side of that wall. Nobody was allowed on the gym floor.

"Before the first fight with Ali, the sports artist LeRoy Neiman asked me if he could come into the gym for a few days and sketch Joe at work. He was a good guy, so I told Joe and he said yes. The next day, Yank comes to me and asks me who he is. I told him and then he said, 'Well, if he draws, why is he taking notes? I want him out of here.' It took me a week to get Neiman back in the gym.

"But the relationship between Joe and Yank grew stronger every day. It was like father and son. And when there was too much to do, Yank brought in Eddie Futch and that was nearly as strong. If Yank had told Joe to jump off the Ben Franklin Bridge, he woulda jumped and never asked why."

Meanwhile, Frazier got better and better. He ran his unbeaten streak to 15–0, including a split decision over hard-punching Oscar Bonavena, who knocked him down twice. That fight certified both Frazier's heart and his chin. Soon after, however, there came a moment that fed into the beliefs of his detractors that Frazier just might not be ready for a championship fight. In some ways, it was attributed to Durham's greatest achievement as a matchmaker. He took Frazier to California and put him up against a sometime sparring partner and full-time club fighter named George "Scrap Iron" Johnson on May 4, 1967.

Frazier did not knock Johnson out. Hell, he didn't even knock him down. The fight went ten rounds, and the final decision to Frazier against a journeyman who had lost half of his thirty fights shook the confidence of a few investors and delighted the prospects of a press corps looking for flaws. However, Durham got what he wanted out of it. He had his guy in with a light-hitting opponent who couldn't hurt him but who, as a wise and older gym fighter, showed Frazier some things he hadn't seen before. It was the ultimate learning experience.

Nobody else paid much attention to that fight. Two months earlier, Muhammad Ali had stopped veteran Zora Folley in Madison Square Garden in the seventh round. The morning after that fight, I was with a half dozen sports writers gathered in Ali's room at Loews Midtown Hotel for a post-mortem.

We had a bigger story than we expected. The pressure had mounted on the champion. It was now clear that he would not step forward in two months and take the oath of induction into the armed services. This was a very different Ali than the one we had previously known.

"Fellas," he said, "don't be asking who I'm gonna fight next. Right now I'm gettin' ready for a much bigger fight. You know if I thought that my goin' to Vietnam would help any of the millions of black people in this country, you wouldn't have to send for me. I'd go. But it won't. Goin' to war with those people ain't gonna help my people one bit. I'll go to jail first."

It was clear to those of us who heard the tone in his voice and saw the look in his eyes that he meant every word. Ali proved it by refusing to step forward at the draft board in Houston. He was stripped of his title by every boxing governing body. The World Boxing Association (WBA) announced it would hold a tournament to choose the next champion. The New York State Athletic Commission said it was smarter, and set up its own elimination match.

Yank Durham saw no value to the WBA eliminations and announced that Joe Frazier would not choose to enter. After all, there were easier pickings elsewhere. The guy whom Frazier had bitterly referred to as "that fat boy" in the Olympic trials had, himself, turned pro under the tutelage of Cus D'Amato. Mathis won twenty-three fights in a row. Like Durham, D'Amato saw the potential storyline in a winner-take-all box-off involving the two protagonists most prominent in the run-up to the 1964 Olympics.

Madison Square Garden, metaphorically called the Mecca of Boxing, had since moved its operations down Eighth Avenue from 49th Street to the above-ground portion of Penn Station. What better attraction than a world title fight to open the new building? So, the management created its own world title. It matched Frazier and Mathis for the world heavyweight championship of New York and Massachusetts.

Mathis had the same overstuffed body. He was surprisingly nimble for a fat heavyweight, but alarmingly vulnerable to body blows. Meanwhile, Durham knew he had the king of all body punchers, and so did that portion of the world who gambles. It made Frazier a 2–1 favorite.

The night held no surprises, neither in nor out of the building. Out on the street, a fairly sizable group of pickets carried signs protesting the exile of Muhammad Ali. Inside the building, a near-capacity crowd saw Mathis box and Frazier walk through his jab. In the eleventh round, the sum total of body blows turned Mathis into a semi-ambulatory heavy bag. The left hook never missed and never stopped. Frazier won by knockout.

Eventually, Frazier would stop Jimmy Ellis, the ersatz WBA champ, easily in four rounds. Once again, heavyweight boxing had a single and highly competent heavyweight champion. But to millions of Americans, nothing was settled as long as Muhammad Ali was denied his right to work.

Four months after Ali had been barred back in 1967, my old friend Willie Gilzenbeg purchased a controlling interest in a welterweight named Sweet Herbie Lee. Gilzenberg had been out of boxing for a decade and wanted me to go down to Baltimore with him to see Lee's first fight under his management. Within two rounds, I suggested to Gilzenberg that Lee would do well to go back to his day job.

However, something else happened during a four-rounder on the undercard that night. It caused me to recall the prophetic words of Muhammad Ali shortly after he refused induction in the draft. "You all ain't done with me yet," he told me. "I will haunt every boxing club and arena in America. Mark my words, they will be aware of my ghost." As I was watching this four-round fight and trying to stay awake, I was jarred back to reality by the roar of a pretty good-sized crowd. Until that moment, the fight had been a monument to passive resistance. But suddenly, the terribly inept fighter stuck his chin out at the other terribly inept fighter and tried to piston his feet into an imitation of the Ali shuffle. The crowd cheered wildly, and I thought to myself: *Ali didn't exaggerate. Like him or despise him, he was tap dancing across the backroads of America's collective mind and would keep on truckin' until he returned to center stage.*

Of course, that would happen primarily because You-Know-Who kept on stirring the pot with a passion that would have left P. T. Barnum mute. And Frazier wanted that fight as much as Ali did—Ali made sure of that. At the time, Ali was trying to make a living with college lectures, and he had moved to Philadelphia. When Frazier stopped Ellis for the WBA title, Ali saw the fight on closed circuit television in a local movie theater. When it ended, he jumped into an aisle and thundered at the crowd, "I am officially starting my comeback. I want that Joe Frazier now."

His next move was to volunteer an interview to a Philadelphia radio station in which he forcefully proclaimed, "Joe Frazier is a clumsy fighter, a coward, and an Uncle Tom."

Finally, he shocked everyone in the Cloverlay Gym and half the cops in Philly by leading a march of a couple hundred people down there and, once denied admission, running from window to window, banging the glass with his fists, and demanding that Frazier come out and fight. Frazier was only too willing to accommodate him. If not for Durham getting between him and the exit, he would have.

In the meantime, they continued on separate highways that would eventually bring them to their moment of truth. Ali traveled the whole country seeking some state that would reinstate his right to be a boxer. In Arizona, a Native American tribe said it would build a small stadium on reservation land and license him to fight a rematch with Zora Folley, an Arizona resident who had been his last opponent. The Native Americans would put up nothing else, keep the live gate, and let Ali and Folley share in the theater-TV revenue. However, an anonymous phone call to the Tribal Council from an official at what was then the Federal Department of Health, Education, and Welfare indicated that such an agreement might impact negatively on various anti-poverty programs the tribe was then receiving from the government.

The Native Americans backed off.

When the news of that near-miss appeared in the media, hustlers from everywhere came out of the woodwork to claim they had the connections to get him a fight. These proved to be more sound and fury than reality. Even Cus D'Amato got into the act with a plan straight out of the Never-Never Land playbook. He wanted to rent an ocean liner, anchor it just outside the United States territorial waters, and televise it.

Just when it appeared that Ali's career was over, a genuine offer seemed possible. Gene Kilroy, who was his business manager and old friend, went down to Mississippi armed with a plan that could get Ali a sanctioned fight and help seriously distressed citizens at the same time. Hurricane Camille had just slammed across Mississippi with a ferocity that had devastated the entire state in August 1969. It had hammered across the state, producing twenty-four-foot-high storm surges and eleven inches of rain, leaving much of Hancock County under fifteen feet of water.

Gene Kilroy met with Governor John Bell Williams in the state capital of Jackson, where they agreed on the following plan. An Ali fight would be licensed by the governor (there was no boxing commission) and all of the live gate money would go to the Salvation

Army for flood relief. The fighters would share the television revenue. Critical to Williams was the role of the Salvation Army as a buffer between the anti-Ali feeling in that state and the good the fight could do for its distressed people. He planned a joint press conference, relying on the charity's role to defeat any criticism. Before he could hold that press conference, the story leaked and the opposition mobilized a vocal response. In the end, Williams had to back down.

However, a Georgia State senator named Leroy Johnson read about Kilroy's attempts and eventually found the loophole that would set Ali free. Ironically, he learned that his own state, where the governor had earlier denied Ali the right to fight, did not have a state boxing commission and could neither authorize nor deny a license application. Johnson was not without influence. He was the first African American to serve as a senator in the state house since reconstruction. He secured the votes in Atlanta, and the city created an official City of Atlanta Boxing Commission. As its first act, it approved a Muhammad Ali–Jerry Quarry fight for the night of October 26, 1970.

Meanwhile, Frazier did not alter his agenda. He went to Detroit to fight Bob Foster, a light heavyweight champion, and hit him so hard in the second round that Foster broke his ankle as he landed.

No heavyweight champion had been faced with what Ali was going through. Gone for three years, weighed down by legal matters, and harassed by both the State Department and the Department of Justice, it was now his time to, once again, prove himself by starting to fish—or forever be consigned to cutting bait.

I remember sitting in the primitive locker room in Atlanta where Ali trained for the Quarry fight. The shower behind us was leaking. The wooden bench we sat on was rickety. Ali reached over, tapped my head, and said, "When I met you, you had a lot more hair." I laughed and replied, "When I met you, you didn't have a spare tire around your waist. You know you only got ten days to get it off."

Ali was magnificent in Atlanta. The venue was the old municipal City Auditorium. Ali fought a brilliant and dominating first round.

His jab was a piston, never missing. However, at the bell he dragged himself back to the corner with his belly heaving like a beached whale. He was fortunate that the cut over Quarry's eye later forced Quarry to concede in the third round.

Ali was smart enough to know that the exile had cost him. He realized he had to have another fight before he tangled with Frazier. And he had to have it quickly because it was felt, in a lot of quarters, that the government wasn't done with him yet. The chosen opponent was a wild-swinging, power-punching free spirit from Argentina named Oscar Bonavena. It was Bonavena who gave Ali his toughest test, nearly knocking him out of the ring and taking Ali the full fifteen rounds to win a decision.

It was a hell of a fight, appreciated by a Madison Square Garden crowd of people who knew what they were seeing, though celebrities had yet to anoint Ali with their presence at ringside. The boxing-savvy crowd understood that the fifteenth-round left hook with which Ali knocked Bonavena down may have been the best punch he ever threw.

Now the road was clear. The fight America wanted would happen, and the nation seemed to have never waited for any other athletic event with such passion. Unwittingly, both Ali and Frazier had been translated into symbols by people who really didn't have a clue how the two fighters felt.

America was being divided by the Vietnam War as never before: hippies who were against it—and thus Ali supporters—were pitted against hard hats who were for it. African Americans who were heavily for Ali as their black hero didn't stop to realize that Ali at the time was opposed to the racial integration that most of them prized, while Frazier was for it. At the same time, many whites who disliked Ali on racial grounds treated Frazier as their designated black representative. Finally, misdirected white people seemed to be split generationally: most of the older ones supported Frazier, and the younger ones of military age rooted for Ali. Each of these groups seemed to forget that, as dramatic as the story was, this was still just a prize fight between two very good heavyweight boxers.

Black Sports Magazine featured a headline asking, "Is Joe Frazier Really a White Man in Black Skin?" Major syndicated columnists such as Red Smith and Jimmy Cannon ripped Ali for refusing to be drafted. And Dick Young, the lead columnist for the *New York Daily News*, who had never served in the military, trumpeted almost daily that Ali had no place in "his" vision of the real America.

One thing all of America agreed upon: They had to fight. But who could put this moment together who didn't already have an axe to grind in this divided country? The answer was the least likely pair of promoters in boxing history—a Hollywood hustler with the gift of gab and a Canadian millionaire with a Forbes-certified bank account.

Jerry Perenchio was a Hollywood agent known primarily on a national basis for his prominent clients: stars like Richard Burton, Elizabeth Taylor, Andy Williams, and Elton John. Time would prove him to be a serious visionary, as he would springboard off this fight of the century to become a billionaire entrepreneur. Back then, he already had the contacts and the vision. What he needed to make this fight was money. Warner Brothers offered to partner with him for a 65–35 split, so he kept on searching.

Long before Jack Kent Cooke's run as a millionaire ended, he would build the LA Forum and FedEx Field in Maryland, as well as own the Lakers, the Redskins, the Kings, and even a pro soccer team called the LA Wolves. Now, he would be the angel in Perenchio's star-studded plan.

The fighters had been offered a five-million-dollar split down the middle. Cooke wanted to stage it in his LA Forum, but Frazier balked. Cooke and Perenchio finally agreed to use Madison Square Garden. After years of waiting and anticipation, it was game on.

No matter what Perenchio did from here on, he couldn't lose. America had not waited this long and yearned this seriously for a heavyweight fight since it had waited for Billy Conn and Joe Louis to come home from war. Artistically, that fight was a massive disappointment, though it did well financially. However, its profit was simply peanuts compared to what awaited Perenchio and Cooke. It was the bright, shining era of theater TV, which hadn't existed when Louis fought. The Fight of the Century, as it was nicknamed, was in full swing, and a positive tsunami of money awaited these co-promoters.

Perenchio, who thought more in star-power terms than those of boxing fans, immediately announced that his Hollywood pal, Burt Lancaster, would do the color commentary on the telecast. He also wanted Andy Williams, a pop singer and, coincidentally, his client, on the show. Logic finally deterred the second choice, but Lancaster was retained, and he probably did the worst telecast in the history of sports. Fortunately, the veteran Don Dunphy provided the blow-by-blow.

Looking back, another sidelight comes to mind. When Ali had made his comeback in Atlanta, I remember standing in the circular driveway that fronted the Hyatt Hotel, looking in amazement at about ten or fifteen sleek limousines that were parked there a week before the fight. Freddie Guinyard, a friend of Joe Louis who ran an after-hours joint in Detroit, noted my puzzlement. "Let me explain," he said, and he began to point at the cars. "Numbers, Detroit; Girls, LA; Drugs, New York City. It's not what you might think. These people don't give a shit about Ali. All they care about is that he beat The Man [the government], which is something they've tried to do all their lives, and that's cool with them."

Some of them were there on the night Ali and Frazier finally fought. They couldn't be missed. They were the men in fur coats, accompanied by eye candy ladies who seemed to have forgotten half their clothes. Additionally, ringside was awash in celebrities who had ostensibly come to see and, more accurately, to be seen. Some were fueled by voyeurism, some by political ideology, and some (nowhere near the majority) because they were genuine fight fans. It was a night when the ghost of Jack Johnson, the great African American heavyweight champion who, like Ali, had been exiled, seemed as much a part of the excitement as the army of militant gawkers outside the Garden and all those closed circuit viewers who wore their raw emotions on their sleeves in theaters from Maine to Southern California.

How could it be otherwise? Here was Muhammad Ali, trying to prove you *could* go home again, despite a tidal wave of logic that the lost time in exile and the haste in scheduling the fight otherwise indicated. And here was Joe Frazier, fueled by white hot anger at the protagonist who had humiliated him with words, who had publicly called him ignorant and mocked his speech patterns. Here was Frazier, who had actually petitioned commissions to let Ali fight again. What had started as a public demand to see them fight had erupted into a war of words between the two, with Ali even calling Frazier an Uncle Tom. Ali's words, as usual, had been inspired by his innate ability to manipulate opponents. Frazier's were reactive and stoked by pure rage.

It was March 8, 1971. You could feel it all in the building. The crowd, like the country, was sharply split between the fighters and the ideologies each (involuntarily) represented, and the noise level seemed to make the building vibrate. At the beginning of the fight, Ali looked as though he had never been away. His portion of the crowd, clearly long-time citizens of Ali Nation, greeted what they saw with a roar. Ali was up on his toes, the tassels on his boxing shoes seeming to fly with each step, and it was jab . . . jab . . . jab, followed by ditto . . . ditto . . . ditto. The rhythm of the combination played like a long-lost concerto.

But not for long. Frazier dropped a falling safe on it. The left hook, that magnificent punch that always seemed to have a will of its own when Frazier fought, hammered Ali into retreat. It was a sign of things to come.

Hooks thrown in multiples sent Frazier ahead on the scorecards. Midway through the fight, he twice hurt Ali with them, but on both occasions Ali, substituting guile for muscle, survived. Each time he was in trouble, he laughed and wobbled his knees, totally fooling Frazier with the gesture. Frazier admitted afterward that he thought Ali was trying to lure him into a trap, causing him to pull back. In fact, he had been duped. The truth was that Ali was hurt on each occasion—badly. He had really staggered, not as a trick as Frazier had thought but rather out of pain. Each time, Ali conned Frazier into caution and survived.

Through it all, the highly divided crowd of partisans saw what it chose to see and believed what it chose to believe. Everybody in the joint thought his or her man was winning. When the bell rang for round fifteen, Angelo Dundee pulled Ali's head close and shouted in his ear, "You're blowing it, son. You got to knock him out to win."

They touched gloves in the center of the ring, and Ali, who was generally not a power puncher, immediately tried to set Frazier up for the knockout he needed with a desperate fusillade of punches. He had a seven-inch reach advantage and believed he could stop Frazier enough to drop him. His punches began to come in bunches, and with each one the crowd reacted. He was superb in that moment, jabbing over and over, throwing an occasional one-two.

Ali was clearly winning the round, and everyone could see that. What they couldn't see or expect was something Frazier told me a week or so after the fight. Ali used to say to me that he never spoke to an opponent in the ring except for the night he taunted Ernie Terrell; however, Frazier told me a different story. "He was throwin' a lot of punches, and he was screaming at me, 'Fool, don't you know that God has ordained I be champion? Don't you know you can't defeat God, chump?' And then he threw a right hand at me, and I ducked and I threw the hook, and I yelled back, 'Well, God's gonna get his ass whipped tonight'—and that's when he went down."

And so did all hope of winning for Ali. He was up immediately, but with a 10–8 round against him, he was clearly doomed. Those numbers should have been reversed if he was to stand any chance.

The knockdown was decisive, though Frazier would have won anyway. Ali being Ali, he decided to re-score the fight. He went on every late night show and convinced the late night audiences otherwise. He said it was a white man's decision.

Two weeks later, Frazier sat next to the ring at Cloverlay Gym, the bitterness obvious. A floor-to-ceiling blow-up of a photo with Ali on the canvas was on the wall behind him. The gym's speaker system was blaring out a song called "Living in the Ghetto."

"He runs his mouth," Frazier said. "I don't mind that. But he said he was going to give me an old-fashioned ghetto whipping. He don't even know what a ghetto is. When I was seven, I was working on a farm. When I was thirteen, I was doing day long man's work. A couple of years later, I was married with kids. When those millionaires were pampering him, I was working in a slaughterhouse. You know what goes on in those places. He never worked. He never had a job. He don't know nothin' about stuff like that. He don't know nothin' about me. And now people are gonna tell me that I'm not the champion?"

But they did.

We went out to eat, and while we stood in front of a deli, three little kids came running up. One of them said, "My daddy says Muhammad Ali was drugged."

Anger flashed in Joe's Frazier's eyes. "Go home and tell your daddy he is right. He was drugged. I drug him with a left hook."

As they ran off, he looked at me and said, "You were there. You saw the fight. You know I won. So what I got to do to convince everyone? What the hell I got to do?"

It was a question that had no answer.

FIVE

Under an African Moon

"Down goes Frazier . . . down goes Frazier."
—*Howard Cosell's frenetic call at ringside*

"I didn't see Foreman as being special. Big, strong, young, and ambitious—yes, all of that. But beatable just the same."
—*Joe Frazier in his autobiography, Smokin' Joe*

W hat's the point of this rematch without a title?" asked a reporter at the weigh-in for Ali–Frazier II. Ali replied, "They really want to see me, but without him there they ain't got nothin' to see."

The people demanded it. The fighters yearned for a rematch. Ali supporters could not accept the clear fact that Frazier had truly beaten him. Frazier's supporters could not accept their denials. Both fighters' worlds had drastically changed since the night they fought for the first time.

For one thing, Joe Frazier no longer held the title he had won from Ali. It now belonged to George Foreman, who had knocked Frazier out in a monumental upset in Jamaica on January 22, 1973.

For another, two years earlier the Supreme Court had changed the course of Ali's life when it orchestrated a strange conclusion to the government's draft evasion case against him. Had that not happened, Ali might well have been in prison instead of returning to the ring.

The Supreme Court deliberations began with an ironic deadlock, many years after the arguments had bounced around in the lower courts and was finally brought to the justices in 1971. Justice Thurgood Marshall abstained because he had been an official in the Department of Justice when the Ali case began. Without him, the votes were deadlocked at 4–4. That no-decision would have sent Ali to jail, but after intense discussion Justice Stewart proposed a compromise. To ensure the case would set no precedent even though Ali would be set free, they threw it out on a technicality. They agreed that the ambiguity of the FBI accusation never made it clear why the examiner's recommendation had been ignored. Ali's conviction was overturned by a unanimous 8–0.

Looking back, I have reason to believe the government went out of its way to deny Ali his rights. By law, the process has two phases: The FBI files a report, and a government-appointed hearing officer files his own conclusions. In almost every case, the examiner's opinion prevails—but not in this one.

Ali's examiner was Lawrence Grauman, a retired Kentucky judge with twenty-five years' experience. After a long and intense interview with Ali, Grauman had written the following opinion: "I recommend that the registrant's claim for conscientious objector status be sustained." But the government had its own agenda. Unlike Grauman, it did not interview Ali, his mother, or his minister. Its report appears to have been based on innuendo, indictment of the Nation of Islam (to which Ali then belonged), and information that remained anonymous. Grauman, a Kentuckian with a sterling reputation as a jurist in Ali's hometown of Louisville, was put under intense pressure to agree with the FBI. I have to give him a place in my private pantheon of heroes when I was a guest on the Dick Cavett television show. When I started talking about Ali, the producer signaled

Cavett to go to an immediate commercial break. We were told that Grauman's son was on the telephone; they had booked him into the show. Grauman's son told a national audience about the pressures his father had been under after ruling for Ali, suggesting that Ali was not the only victim in the case.

Meanwhile, the heavyweight picture had its own surprising twist. In a title defense, Frazier was totally demolished by George Foreman. He was knocked down six times, causing Foreman to holler at Yank Durham, Frazier's trainer, "Stop it, or I'm going to kill him." Finally, the referee, Arthur Mercante, stopped the fight. Frazier didn't make it out of the second round.

It was an upset that rocked the boxing world. A decade later, Foreman explained how we all should have seen it coming. By then, he had lost his own title, retired, and then come back at an advanced age, on the verge of winning it back.

"It's simple," he told me. "Styles dictate every fight. I never had trouble punching down to a shorter man. The uppercuts were the reason. I could fight Joe a hundred times and probably beat him ninety-nine. But I could fight Muhammad a hundred times and he'd probably beat me ninety-nine. Yet when Joe and Muhammad fought each other, trust me, it would have been life and death a hundred times. Styles make that happen."

Frazier's loss to Foreman threatened to disrupt all of Ali's comeback plans. Yes, he wanted revenge, but the title was an even bigger motivation. On the way to Frazier, Ali had fought a little known ex-marine named Ken Norton, whose style was awkward but whose punching power was without question. Norton broke Ali's jaw and won the fight, dealing Ali his second defeat on March 31, 1973.

Now, Ali needed to fight Frazier just to keep on keepin' on. However, this time it was as though it were being contested on an alien planet. It took a lot of fights nobody cared about to keep him moving back to center stage. What happened to the beautiful people who had scrambled to be a part of Ali–Frazier I? You could almost hear them saying, "Don't you remember, dear? We saw that movie

years ago." They were replaced by the smallest celebrity row since
St. Nicholas Arena in New York held club fights. There was Barbra
Streisand and George Jessel, surrounded by a B-list of the usual suspects in search of free tickets. Gone were the celebrities and their
desperation to be seen on fight night. Gone were the street hustlers
in their furs and the underdressed eye candy they had brought with
them. Gone was the ringside camera of Frank Sinatra, that one time
he pretended to be a professional photographer at Ali–Frazier I and
had a shot published in *Life* magazine.

Gone, too, was the dynamic duo of Jerry Perenchio and Jack Kent
Cooke. They had obtained a rematch contract before the first fight
that read the two would meet again with the heavyweight title at stake.
But now, neither had a title. The contract was null and void. Madison
Square Garden rushed in and took over the promotion, which marked
the formal return of a *real* fight crowd in the old fight arena to witness
what it recognized as two true fighters battling their hearts out. Madison
Square Garden's ringside once again became a place fit for cigar smoke.

One more thing hadn't changed. The animosity between Ali
and Frazier had not abated. It was alive, strong, and very much in
evidence in a television interview with Howard Cosell a couple of
days before the fight. Ali unleashed his usual verbal broadside against
Frazier, who clearly began to bristle. Then Rachman Ali, Ali's brother,
who did not belong in the room, entered and walked menacingly toward Frazier. Frazier thought Rachman was going to hit him, and Ali
thought Frazier was going to hit Rachman. The fighters immediately
grappled and each hit the floor. Security raced in and Cosell beamed,
the thought of television ratings dancing inside his head.

They fought on a Monday night on January 28, 1974. It wasn't
the same. Hell, three years away can do that to your dance team; now
consider eight. Ali was up on his toes punching, throwing combinations, landing blows. A few years earlier, the sequence would have
been followed by blood. The jabs would have cut, the short right
hands would have jolted. But they didn't that day, and Frazier answered with two hooks without even backing up. However, Frazier,

too, had become a different fighter. In the next round, he came tearing out and unleashed the big hook. In the past, it would have been followed by another one and another one and another one. But on this night, he delivered one punch and reloaded.

Ali won by unanimous decision. I had Frazier winning the twelve-rounder 6–5–1, but the rounds were close and I had no quarrel. It seemed to me and my colleagues at ringside that it was over for both of them. In the same way that we had thought about Sonny Liston, we agreed that George Foreman would be champion for at least fifty years. Eighteen months later, Ali would fool us again.

Meanwhile, at least, the truth about Foreman was that while he could knock down the wall of your choice, he was still learning to fight at that point. As a troubled youth in Houston's bloody fifth ward, he had probably been saved from only-Lord-Knows-What when he agreed to join the Job Corps. As luck would have it, my future brother-in-law was stationed with him in California.

The recreation director was a man named Doc Broadus, who discovered early on that Foreman, with his strength and size, could be taught to box. In his search for sparring partners, he had few takers. One day, he said to my future brother-in-law, Leon Leach, "Come on. Get in the ring for a couple of minutes with George. He'll just block what you throw. He won't hit you."

"You got that right," Leon told him. "I'm outta here. Go find some other idiot."

Later, Leon saw him on the televised 1968 Olympics from Mexico. "The way he hit that guy, I just knew if I'd gone in there to accommodate Doc, I would have been taking my meals for ten years through a straw."

The thing that most impressed me about Foreman on the day I finally interviewed him in California was the way he dominated a room. Here was a guy wearing bib overalls, a huge man who, in those days, spoke with a deceptive lisp.

"I've seen you cut off a ring," I told him, "and I'm impressed."

"Well," he replied, "somebody told me he ain't gonna run. Somebody told me he's gonna stand and fight. Bad for him. Real bad for him. I don't care what he does. I'll cut off the ring and then cut off his neck."

A week later, Ali asked me, "What's he gonna do? Bring a pair of scissors?"

Physically and rhetorically, it was now game on at a time when a lot of us thought we might not see Ali again. We should have known better. Ali's philosophy was lifted directly from a fellow I consider the Poet Laureate of Baseball. His name was Yogi Berra, and as most of the world knows, he was the guy who said with total logic about any contest: "It ain't over until it's over."

We had written Ali off eighteen months after he had convinced us all that, in beating Joe Frazier, he had looked like a living relic of an era we thought was over. But what did we know? Hell, when it came to Muhammad Ali, what did any of us know? Least cautious of all was George Foreman, who was younger, bigger, and stronger than Muhammad Ali, but, as we came to learn in the pre-dawn of an African day in 1974, was surely not smarter.

Because of the fight in which he broke Ali's jaw, Ken Norton had become the logical contender before Ali could muscle his way into a title shot against Foreman. So Foreman agreed to first defend his title against Norton in Caracas, Venezuela. If Foreman won, the stage would be set for an Ali–Foreman fight that, as time would later tell, would take place down by the banks of the Zaire river on the edge of a city called Kinshasa, an ocean away in Africa. When Norton finally retired, his fight record bore witness to the fact that big punchers seemed to have their way with him—and Foreman was a very big puncher. However, Norton *could* also punch—Ali's time taking meals through a straw after their first fight was proof of that.

For a long time, the veteran trainer Eddie Futch had been both Norton's and Frazier's trainer, dividing his time between both of them. Frazier trained on the East Coast and Norton on the West. When Bob Biron, Norton's manager, demanded that Futch make a choice, much to Norton's disadvantage and possibly the reason for his decline later in his career, Futch chose Frazier.

The night of Foreman–Norton on March 26, 1974, my seat in the press row was next to Futch. The fight was even for a round. Then Foreman, a tremendous puncher, landed a jab on the side of Norton's skull. Futch leaned over toward me, and all he said was, "Uh oh . . . fight over." He was right. Norton's legs began to wobble. Knocked down three times, he never got out of the second round.

On the flight to Caracas, I had sat with promoter Don King, the man who would eventually change the geography of modern-day boxing. It was our first meeting. I wondered what his role with the broadcasting company Video Techniques was, and he told me, "I am the company's black interface." When asked the same question on the way home, he replied, "I am the company's president." It was incredible how swiftly the American Dream moved through its work—but not once you understood the moves behind it.

Don King, a former Cleveland numbers czar, was a man convicted and imprisoned for killing a street person who had welched on a debt. He once told me, "I don't worry about the kind of competition I have in boxing. Like Victor Hugo, I tell the enemy, 'Send me giants to fight.'" King himself was a genuine giant in his own right. He was the one who obtained the signed contracts from Ali and Foreman; without him, the fight would have been impossible.

However, it wasn't easy. King's hunt for money was more difficult than getting the fighters' signatures. First, he had to promise Ali and Foreman five million dollars each. Now, all he needed was the money to back it up.

Few people know what happened next. The future of Ali–Foreman, the future of Don King, and the future of the strangest sports event on the planet all turned on a single telephone call from Zaire (known today as the Democratic Republic of Congo). A mid-level employee of the Zaire Government telephoned Herbert Muhammad,

Ali's manager, in Chicago and dropped a bomb. "We want this fight to be held in our country," he said. Herbert called King and Hank Schwartz, the other man behind Video Techniques, and the race for funding was on.

First, they recruited a filmmaker from England named John Daly, who supplied the walking-around money for the promoter's quest for the whole bundle. Next came an international finance hustler named Frederick Weymar, who worked with other people's money. Throughout the day leading up to the fight, Weymar was seen in the presence of members of the power hierarchy in Zaire. It was said that he was a friendly conduit to bankers in Switzerland, where Mobutu Sese Seko, the dictator of Zaire, kept his private funds (and where some of the fight money wound up).

Mobutu was nobody to mess with. Among his many "credits" was a kidnapping that led to the murder of the country's first prime minister, Patrice Lumumba, which paved the way to Mobutu's rise to power. Virtually all of Mobutu's political ascent was marked by his personal elimination of everyone who stood in his way. The final source of funding came from the Risnala Investing Company, a shell that had been sold three times from Panama, where it was chartered and passed off by its shadowy owners as great investors in Zaire. Even today, nobody is quite sure of its role, but then nobody was about to ask the inscrutable and ruthless President for Life, either.

The man who was deputized as Mobutu's public face for the fight was named Mandungu Bula. While Bula's mouth may have moved on its own, it was Mobutu's words that came out. At a dinner in Paris where they met, Bula asked Don King about the situation.

"The situation," King said, "is that you are getting the biggest event in the history of sports."

"But you are with Jews in your company. Can you trust them, brother?"

"You can trust one," King said of Schwartz. "He is a brilliant man," Bula replied, "I shall tell my president that I have found a strong black man."

And so it was that Ali was vindicated as a prophet, King was certified as the new power in boxing, and Foreman was launched on a perilous journey that seemed as much science fiction as boxing—assuming there is a difference.

The week before I left for Central Africa, I sat on a bench outside the United Nations complex in New York with Tshimpupu wa Tshimpupu, Bula's fight press liaison. The conversation only heightened what I perceived to be the romance inherent in traveling to such an exotic locale to write about a sports event that, from the crudest of crumbling stadiums in Kinshasa, would be beamed to the world by what was then the most sophisticated of satellites.

I knew little about Zaire other than that it had been the Belgian Congo, then the Democratic People's Republic of the Congo, and under Colonel Joseph Mobutu had been named Zaire. I was also aware that it was there that a nineteenth-century journalist named Henry Stanley had focused much of his search for a missing British explorer, a journey that, legend has it, dramatically ended with the words, "Dr. Livingstone, I presume."

Even though Tshimpupu was a political hack attached to the Zairian UN delegation, he knew how to push a writer's emotional buttons. When he told me the ring would be pitched not far from the spot where Stanley had passed and that among Zaire's ethnic groups were the Pygmies, he convinced me that this was a story in search of an author.

Almost as an afterthought, I asked him to tell me a little about Colonel Joseph Mobutu.

"Our president is now named Mobutu Sese Seko," he said. "He has built a nation for his children with hospitals and schools and television. He has given us pride. You must always honor his proper name."

Actually, the name and title Mobutu had given himself was President Mobutu Sese Seko Kuku Wa Za Banga of Zaire, which translates to "The all-powerful warrior who, because of his endurance and inflexible will to win, will go from conquest to conquest leaving fire in his wake."

Even that was incomplete. In addition to his "endurance and inflexible will to win," there was also his ability to murder, steal, and maintain happy ties with the CIA. He had already been fingered by Amnesty International for the torture of political prisoners and had not hesitated to support episodes of strategic genocide in neighboring Rwanda when it served his purpose.

When Ali took me to meet him, dark glasses shielded Mobutu's eyes. Knowing what I knew by then, it was clear they were not the windows of whatever passes for a soul. Some five hundred yards away from the palace—away from the solid gold leopard cages, away from the excessive opulence—shoeless children with bloated bellies surrounded us. For me, the whole agonizing spectrum of the history of Mobutu's Zaire could be measured by those five hundred yards.

But that day, October 30, 1974, the fight itself remained an electric story of romance, history, and justice deferred and finally obtained. In many ways, it is the benchmark of Ali's career. It generated staggering myths through phony books by people who weren't there or who had simply passed through.

Zaire—roughly the size of that portion of the United States east of the Mississippi River—is a polyglot of more than twenty tribes with nothing in common, including their native tongues (other than the fact that somebody long ago claimed the whole land mass for Belgium), who communicate with each other through a hybrid mercantile language known as Lingala, a kind of African Yiddish.

It was chaos from the moment the outside world arrived. As they got off the plane, Ali asked Gene Kilroy, a majordomo of the Ali camp, "Who do these people hate?"

"I couldn't say 'white people,'" Kilroy explained, "because I was white and so was Angelo Dundee. So I said, 'I guess the Belgians,' who had occupied the country.

"So there was this scene. Thousands of people chanting, 'Ali!' and then the cry changed to 'Ali, *boom-a-yay*' [in Lingala] and the interpreter told me it means, 'Ali, kill him.' Ali turned that into an everyday chant inside George Foreman's head.

"Anyway, it was getting very dark and the noise got even louder, and suddenly Ali raised his hands and got total silence. Then he announced, 'George Foreman is a Belgian.'

"In my view, in that instant, Africa began to clutter George Foreman's thinking."

Kilroy jumped in with both feet. He went to the American Embassy and secured the right for the camp to do all food shopping at the American commissary. He got the embassy to clear all passports and visas for his camp and the visiting journalists. Without both concessions, there might not have been a fight.

Meanwhile, Ali went to work as only he could have—he leapfrogged directly into the head of George Foreman. He played Foreman's psyche until it tightened like an overwound violin string, exploiting a myriad of self-doubts that plagued the then-troubled heavyweight champion. Ali nicknamed him "the Mummy," shouting each time he saw him in the days leading up to the fight. "No mummy gonna beat the great Muhammad Ali when we meet in the horror house," he cried.

Ali dug deeply with the words, "George Foreman ain't nothing but a bully." Most of all, he turned the African venue against Foreman, capturing the affections of the people. He even altered genetics, turning Foreman into a white man by carefully explaining to the spectators at one training session: "George come here with a dog. I don't have to tell you all how many dogs were set against you over the years. What kind of a dog did he bring? A Belgian shepherd. And who was it who oppressed you? The Belgians. So what does that make him?"

When Foreman was cut over the right eye after a sparring session, delaying the fight for six weeks, Ali and Kilroy went to Mobutu's people and told them, "George is gonna run away. You better put some army people in front of his hotel." They did, and Foreman began to brood even more deeply after this insult. By fight night, he was a nervous wreck.

Because of time constraints dictated by the orbit of a communications satellite, the fight would not start until 4 a.m. The promoters filled in the gap from midnight forward with traditional native dancers. A full moon hung over the proceedings. And through it all, the steady throb of drums.

As the countdown melted away, I pondered something few others knew. Ali, then thirty-two-years-old, had long suffered from arthritic hands. Painkillers had been a constant companion. Kilroy had taken the biggest single pre-fight step of all. He brought Ali to an orthopedist in Philadelphia named Dr. James Nixon, who ordered him off all of those shots and prescribed hot paraffin soaks for both hands three times a day. The hands began to come around. A month later, the late Jerry Lisker, sports columnist of the *London Sun*, and I journeyed to Deer Lake, Pennsylvania, to watch Ali's final preparations. I couldn't believe what we saw. For the first time in over a year, his hands permitted him to bang away on the heavy bag. With each punch, he chanted, "I'm . . . gonna . . . knock . . . that . . . sucker . . . out."

"I'm picking him by knockout," I told Lisker on the ride home.

"You think he means what he said?"

"I know one thing he said a long time ago to both us. He said, 'If I say a mosquito can pull a plow, don't argue. Hitch him up.'" As I recall, we both picked him by knockout and were the only two who did.

Ultimately, Ali and Foreman fought in a setting that will never be duplicated this side of science fiction. They fought within a few kilometers of the very spot where Henry Stanley found Dr. David Livingstone. They fought in a tired old soccer stadium, home to the Zaire Leopards. They fought under a multi-story portrait of Mobutu. Away from ringside, the lighting was atrocious.

That African night was ebony black and loaded with the kind of stars you only see back home over prairieland. The sound of drums echoed through the night, and then suddenly stopped cold and were replaced by a roaring crescendo of "Ali, *boom-a-yay*" that was repeated over and over, getting louder each time. The crowd came to their feet, still chanting, as Ali came down the aisle and into the ring. It was the perfect setting for what Ali had described to us that morning as "the king going back to Africa to get his crown."

Across the way, Foreman was as tense as a coiled spring. He came through the ropes together with his trainer, Dick Saddler, and his advisor, Archie Moore. Never have I seen three men more alone than this trio, who were friendless in Africa.

Before the referee called both men to the center for final instructions, Ali walked menacingly over to Foreman in the ring. He stood two feet away, screaming, "I'm gonna pop you to death, sucker. Warn all them suckers around you. I'm gonna pop . . . pop . . . *pop* . . . you hear me?" Just before they pulled him away, you could almost see the ferocity that was Foreman's stock in trade evaporate before your eyes.

I do not have to tell you about the rope-a-dope, considerably heightened in effectiveness when Ali elected to lie back on those ropes until the time of his choosing. Others have written about how that was the battle plan—it was not. In the first round, Foreman hit him hard and Ali retreated to the ropes, put his gloves in front of his face, and tried to gain some time to figure it out.

By the end of the first round, Ali had it figured out. Foreman kept trying to ram his gloves with ferocious force between those of Ali's, to no avail. Foreman had never run into anything he wanted to do that he couldn't do in any fight he'd ever had.

Round after round, Ali's corner screamed, "Get off the ropes. Get off the damned ropes." Round after round, Ali ignored. Once, he yelled, "Shut the hell up." He knew what he was doing. Throughout the rounds, he taunted Foreman. "That's all you got? . . . That's the best you have? . . . Keep tryin', sucker." Every once in a while, he would hit back, but not often.

In the eighth round, attrition, fatigue, and frustration set Foreman up for the short right-hand lead that shocked the world. In fact, there were two, but by the time the first landed Foreman was already stumbling and groping to find an invisible handle. He seemed to fall in slow motion. He was so big that it was like watching the collapse of a California Redwood. First, his feet went; then the knees; then all of George. He would later argue that he had beaten the count, but that was empty rhetoric.

Zack Clayton, the referee, raised Ali's hand while half of Zaire seemed to jump into the ring. Then the rain came. We wrote our stories and were trapped in the downpour a half hour after we were done. By then, Ali was long gone into the new dawn.

By the time we returned to our quarters, Ali had been the champion for just a couple of hours. We knew there was still more to be written the next day, so we set out to find him. When we did, he was standing at the edge of the Congo River with his back to us, staring off into the distance in the direction of what was once the French Congo. He stood there a long time. He never told any of us what he was thinking. Framed by the first fresh rays of a new African sunshine, he raised his arms as high as they could go in a sort of victory gesture.

He turned, saw us, and walked slowly toward where we stood. After what seemed like an eternity, he said, "Fellas, you'll never know what tonight means to me."

Maybe it was the smell of the African flowers and a slight breeze that preceded the blazing heat, but in that instant I think I knew what his gesture meant. In that instant he was, indeed, the king who had come home and claimed his crown.

SIX

The Day Nobody Blinked

"It will be a killa and a thrilla and a chilla when
I get the gorilla in Manila."

—*Muhammad Ali*

"I'm tryin' to pay the rent. The kids ain't got no shoes, the
motorcycle is in the shop and the Rolls-Royce needs
a new cigarette lighter."

—*Joe Frazier', responding to the question, "Why are
you going to fight Ali again?"*

O nce again, Muhammad Ali was the king of all heavyweights. The pressure leading up to his conquest of George Foreman had been enormous—now there seemed to be no new giants to slay or mountains to climb. It was time to make a few easy dollars. Don King, with the necessary support from Herbert Muhammad, Ali's manager, had put together the fight in Zaire. He was still in control of promotional rights for the champ (a fragile relationship that Herbert changed from time to time) and wanted to move quickly to continue the cash flow.

On the night Ali stunned the world by knocking out George Foreman, Chuck Wepner was sitting in the Stanley Theater in Jersey City's Journal Square watching the closed circuit telecast of the fight. Don King had promised him the next fight with Foreman. When Foreman hit the canvas, so did Wepner's stomach. *Back to the club fights*, he must have thought. *Just my luck.*

Chuck Wepner was essentially a club fighter; however, nobody who ever paid to see him fight was shortchanged by his determination and aggression. Unfortunately, he was shortchanged by the thinness of his own skin and facial bone structure. Together, they combined to earn him a deserved reputation as what is known in the business as a bleeder.

Even Wepner accepted that fact. As a case in point, during the sixth round of a fight in Madison Square Garden with a college kid named Randy Neuman, there was a violent clash of heads, and when the two fighters stepped back blood was on Wepner's trunks and chest. The referee, Arthur Mercante, stepped in. "Sorry, fellas, but I got to stop this now." When Wepner pleaded for more time, Mercante responded, "Not you, Chuck. It's not your blood. It's his."

For both King and Ali, Wepner was a perfect opponent. However, he wasn't so for the World Boxing Association (WBA). "He's not even ranked," Bob Brennan, the head of the WBA rating committee, said, to which his friend Willie Gilzenberg replied, "Don't say no until you've checked your mail for a couple of days." Gilzenberg, based in Newark, New Jersey, walked across the street to a dollar store and bought a blank award certificate with a phony gold seal on the bottom. He mailed it to Brennan, but not after first filling in the following: "Awarded to Chuck Wepner as the North American Heavyweight Champion." Brennan laughed and said, "Okay. I'll put him in the top ten." The match was made for Don King's hometown of Cleveland on March 24, 1975.

"I had fought twenty-seven times before that and never once had a regular trainer or went to a training camp," Wepner said. "Now King gave me the money for it, so I worked harder than ever before, and I felt I had a puncher's chance with Ali. But I knew he was still Ali."

The fight wasn't close. Though Ali won it with reasonable ease, in the ninth round Wepner landed a right hand to Ali's jaw, and in that instant his lead foot got tangled with Ali's lead foot, tripping Ali and knocking him of balance. Whether it was his fist or his foot, it was a knockdown, and the crowd reacted at a terrific noise level.

"I came back to the corner," Wepner later told me, "and I looked at Braverman [Wepner's trainer] and said, 'Start the car, Al. We're going to the bank. We're rich.'" Braverman replied, "Better look over at him. He's standing waiting for the bell, and he looks really pissed off."

Ali left no doubts, and the referee stopped the fight late into the fifteenth round with Ali declared the winner. That morning, Wepner bought his wife the sexiest negligee he could find, as he told me years later. "You put it on because tonight you sleep with the heavyweight champion of the world," he told her. "Uh, does he come here or do I go to his room?" she replied.

Ali would fight three more times that year. Ron Lyle was a ferocious puncher out of Denver by way of Colorado State Penitentiary. He also had no fear. As the fight wore on, two things happened. Angelo Dundee told Ali, "You're way ahead, way ahead. Don't get careless." Gene Kilroy, Ali's business manager, turned in his seat to Rahman, Ali's brother, and said, "You gotta tell him he's blowing the fight." Rahman immediately jumped into the ring and told his brother, "You blowing it."

Ali knocked Ron Lyle out in the eleventh round. Then he went to Malaysia and fought Joe Bugner in a listless, boring contest outdoors in a hundred degrees, winning it by miles.

Two days before that fight in Malaysia, I had been walking down a hotel hallway with Dave Anderson of *The New York Times* when we heard Ali shouting, "I'll knock him out. I'll knock the sucker out." For the record, Ali had announced his retirement that very afternoon. Both of us walked in through his open door to see what the hell was happening. He was watching a tape of Joe Frazier fighting and jumping up and down, yelling, "Old man . . . can't fight . . . I'll kill him."

"We thought you quit," I said.

"No, just trying to sell tickets. Wait 'til I get my hands on Frazier." Incredibly, that was exactly what was going to happen in a few months' time. But Ali had no idea that this would be the most brutal fight of his career and that, as he wearily left the ring in Manila afterward, he would pause when he reached the press section and tell us through battered and swollen lips, "Fellas, that's the closest you will ever see to death."

At first, that fight on October 1, 1975, in Manila, the Philippines, represented, in Ali's belief, a mismatch against a fighter who had become slower and less active, and whose reflexes seemed to be gone. It all added up to an easy payday.

But to Frazier, it meant a chance to unleash the anger that had been boiling within him for years. It had begun with Ali painting him as an Uncle Tom before their first fight in 1971, and it gained momentum before their second in 1974 when the two grappled on a television studio floor after Ali called him ignorant.

On the way to the press conference in New York to announce Ali–Frazier III, Ali unleashed his most hurtful verbal attack. When he and Gene Kilroy stopped in a Seventh Avenue novelty shop to kill time, he was attracted to a tiny gorilla doll. He erupted into wild laughter and immediately purchased it.

When Ali stepped up to the podium, he held up the little gorilla and punched it repeatedly as he looked at Frazier and shouted, "It will be a killa and a thrilla and a chilla when I get the gorilla in Manila."

After the conference, Frazier told Kilroy, "He went too far this time." Kilroy replied, "One day, we'll all sit on a park bench and laugh at this." "That day will never come," Frazier said, with open anger. Kilroy, Ali's loyal friend, said to me later on, "Muhammad told me he was just trying to sell tickets, but he was wrong. There was no percentage of the gate here. It was a flat out contractual split of a fee."

Frazier went back to Philadelphia to train in the controlled silence of his gym. It was isolated enough to make the new strategy he was about to pursue totally effective. For Frazier's entire career, he had been a brilliant but nevertheless one-trick pony—the left hook was his only weapon. Eddie Futch, his trainer and manager, brought a new face into the command post, George Benton, a Philadelphia legend and brilliant middleweight fighter as intelligent as he was skilled.

"Eddie," Benton told him, "We got to give this boy a right hand. We got to give Ali something very distracting to think about. I can do that."

So the great experiment began, laced with hard work, sweat, and total secrecy. Joe Frazier became a man with a better arsenal than he had ever possessed.

If you believe in omens—I didn't then and still don't—then you might have been misled by the scene in the driveway at the Hyatt Hotel when I arrived in Manila three weeks before the fight. A tall, angular black man, wearing tails and a top hat, and clutching a Bible in his left hand, was hurling the following pronouncements at the doorman: "Look at me, man. I have seen God. He has told me that Joe Frazier is a mighty warrior with the power. You will not see God. You will not go to Heaven. And Joe Frazier will be the Lord's instrument in making a mighty miracle."

At that point, I leaned over to my traveling colleague, Jerry Lisker of the *New York Post*, and said, "Ask the guy if God is willing to lay 8–5 on that."

It was the most commonplace thing to happen that week.

The next morning, it rained. "There will be no roadwork today," Angelo Dundee told Ali. "The hell there won't. Let's take a ride," Ali said. Who else would consider doing his roadwork from behind the wheel of an El Dorado? Soon, the rain stopped. A brace of police motorcyclists pulled alongside. Ali alighted, grabbed one of the cop's helmets, got on his bike, and rode off.

And the day had just begun.

That afternoon in the National Folk Arts Center, Joe Frazier moved across the ring toward a sparring partner, just as a human foghorn shouted down from the rafters, "Go . . . rilllllla. . . . Go . . . rilla." Ali was leaning over a catwalk high above. When the session ended, Frazier said to me, "He certainly acts like he is losing his mind. Do they have some sort of mental health clinic here? I don't want them to throw a net over him before the fight." Later that night, Ali also stood outside the hotel and aimed a toy gun at Frazier, who had just appeared on a balcony above.

The next day, Drew Bundini Brown, the Ali cheerleader who authored the opus "float like a butterfly, sting like a bee," crashed the Frazier camp, offering to bet six grand on his man. From the back of the room, an adolescent voice shouted back, "I'll bet you a hundred." It was Frazier's son, Marvis. Later that day, I asked Brown if he really bet the kid. He responded, "Does a bear crap in the woods? Hell, yes, I bet him and he better pay me when he loses."

This was the way it was from arrival until fight night. Just when we thought all would finally get quiet on the Eastern Front, Ali attended a party thrown by the President of the Philippines, Ferdinand Marcos, bringing along his girlfriend, Veronica Porché. Back in Chicago, Belinda Ali, Ali's wife, remained clueless until she picked up the newspaper the next morning. That afternoon, she jumped on the first thing smoking toward Manila. The marital fight didn't last long. After a screaming, foot-stamping confrontation, Belinda took her leave. It occurred to all of us that this was a hell of a way for Ali to get ready for an opponent like Frazier.

That same day, Frazier sat on a couch in his hotel room, taking our questions. After a while, he stood up, looked at us, and said, "He can't get his mind together. He can't touch me when it comes to ability or decency. I ain't no gorilla. Because of him, my kids come home from school crying because the others kids repeat what he said. I don't want this fight to end early. I wanna punish him; I wanna put it on him." By the end of the interview, we were all convinced that there would be serious business on fight night.

No sports event had ever gripped the Philippines like this one. But then, there had never been a heavyweight championship fight anywhere on the planet to rival that of Muhammad Ali and Joe Frazier.

Two days before the fight, the local paper went off the wall with the news that Eddie Futch had threatened to pull his fighter out unless the local commission listened to his demands about the selection of the referee.

Standing on the corner of the press center at the Bayview Plaza Hotel, Futch told the media that during Ali–Frazier II, referee Tony Perez had permitted Ali to hold behind the neck while he hit Frazier 133 times. "I do not want that style of refereeing. I won't permit it."

"And you know that number how?" I asked him.

"I watched the tape and counted. They gave us three choices. One of them was Zack Clayton. I have seen him sitting at ringside during a fight and rooting for Ali. They ain't gonna push him at me. If it's Clayton, there's no fight."

"Well," I told him, "It's a long swim home."

"I'm serious," he said. "You'll see." What he didn't tell us was that three nights earlier, in a private meeting with President Ferdinand Marcos and Louis Tabuena, the head of the local boxing commission, Futch had expressed the same sentiments and was sure they would accept his complaint. To be on the safe side, he also contacted Philadelphia Mayor Frank Rizzo for help. Frazier was from Philly and so was Clayton, who had a civil service job with the city. Rizzo subsequently told Clayton that if he even went to Manila he would be stealing city time and would be fired.

"They claim a local ref would be too little to separate big men like Joe and Muhammad if they held," Futch said. "Well, I don't care if they choose a sixty-pound dwarf. It ain't gonna be Zack Clayton."

And it wasn't. The referee was a cop from Manila named Sonny Padilla. He looked to be the biggest Filipino this side of Roman Gabriel, the old Los Angeles Rams quarterback. No referee had ever had a more difficult task. After the fight, both fighters said Padilla had done a spectacular job.

The fight was set for 10:45 a.m. inside the aluminum-roofed Araneta Coliseum. The building had no air-conditioning. When the ring and TV lights were turned on, it was 105 degrees inside the ring.

Sitting in the press section, waiting for the fighters to enter the main hall, I noted a huge gold trophy, roughly the size of a center on a Filipino basketball team, sitting up against the wall. It was supposed to give more incentive to each fighter, and President Marcos would present it. After the incredible events that would happen inside the ring that day, I believed presenting it would be like importing coal to West Virginia.

Incentive? Hell, that was the last thing these guys needed. They didn't need Manila, they didn't need a trophy, and they didn't need a world championship belt. As passionate as their rivalry always was and as unforgiving as their assessments of each other would be forever, they knew what they were fighting for.

They were fighting for the world championship of each other, and that kind of performance has never been duplicated since. They could have fought in a phone booth or on a melting ice floe. It was all the room they needed; theirs was an involvement without end. Before this day, on which they wrote their final September Song, it was clear that one's name would never be mentioned without the other. They remained as tightly linked time travelers for decades, even after they left the city of Manila.

It was the greatest fight I ever saw. Hell, I think it was the greatest fight anyone ever saw. Ironically, it began as though it was just going to feature the recitation of tunes of glory for Ali. In the beginning, the crowd oohed and ahed along with the rhythm of his lightning jabs. It seemed every critic in the boxing business was right about the loss of the bounce in Frazier's legs and the toll too many early battles had taken on him.

During the first two rounds, Ali threatened to turn Frazier into a personal heavy bag. However, in the fourth Frazier began to come forward with a new cadence in his steps. Ali was landing, but Frazier was crowding, and soon he had Ali on the ropes and was hammering his body with left hooks. After the end of the round, Ali turned to the crowd, waved his arms, and chanted, "Ali . . . Ali . . . Ali," convinced the inevitable knockout was about to come.

Ali entered the fifth round ready to end it. He was unprepared for what happened next. They exchanged punches—Ali a combination and Frazier a hook—then Frazier did the absolutely unexpected: he hammered a right hand against Ali's head. Astonished by the right hand, he grunted, "You an old man. They told me you washed up. You ain't got no right hand."

"They told you wrong," Frazier said. "Go ask George Benton." Another right cross crashed against Ali's head. Ali retreated to the safety of the ropes until the bell rang.

Between rounds, Dundee screamed at Ali. "Stay off them damned ropes. When he puts you there, spin him and hit him . . . spin him and hit him . . . do you hear me? Stop playing."

But the next few rounds were out of Ali's hands. Fifteen seconds into the seventh, Frazier landed a ferocious left hook. Ali backed up. Frazier continued with a flurry of hooks and, at the end of the round, a thudding hook to the body and another to the head. It appeared to be Frazier's time.

At the start of the eighth, Ali's white trunks started to sag under the burden of his sweat. He began the round with a right-left-right combo to Frazier's head. Slower now, but no less determined, Joe answered with a hook to the head. Frazier held onto control with his own rally in the last fifty seconds that sent Ali back into the ropes again.

As suddenly as the Frazier team experienced elation, it now faced reality at the end of the round. Between rounds, Futch noticed, alarmed, swelling under both of his fighter's eyes. The cut man Pop Bailey worked Frazier's eyes furiously with an endswell. Although Frazier had taken control at this time, unless he scored a knockout soon the swelling would cost him the fight.

They continued. With each punch Frazier landed, Ali came back with a jab combination and Frazier's eyes steadily closed. He was ahead, but he couldn't win. When they had mapped out their battle plan, Futch had said, "Stay low. Make him punch down. Make him throw the punch he doesn't like to throw, the uppercut. When you see he is going to throw it, step in first and throw the hook." The day after the fight, Futch told me, "We had him in the eleventh, but [Ali] is special. He survived and Joe had to straighten up to see. In the twelfth, the eye was closed and Joe couldn't see when Ali's right hand was coming. In the twelfth, I knew it was lost."

Frazier was bleeding from the mouth. Bailey's best efforts couldn't help his vision. Near the end of the twelfth, Ali landed three straight left hands to the face, and Frazier became a lumbering shell of himself. In the next round, Ali knocked out Frazier's mouthpiece. After it was replaced, he connected a right-left-right to the head. Then, as fatigue gripped every muscle, Ali fired another combination that landed squarely, and Frazier was stunned for the first time since the early going.

In that same round, I saw something I had never seen in any ring in my six decades in the business. Frazier was standing with his arms down, his legs wobbling, and his body reeling, fighting the pull of gravity and aching muscles. Ali, just five feet away, stared at him. The champion's legs were like twin pillars caught in quicksand. He couldn't even move forward to end it.

And what could you say about the fourteenth round of the fight? Ali, the consummate pro who knew his job, reached somewhere deep within his bronzed, wet body and fired nine consecutive bullseyes at Frazier's head. Nine with no response. Blood hung in a loose, damp rope from Frazier's mouth. His eyes were glazed. Incredibly, he made it through.

It was clear that the fifteenth round would decide it. I had Ali ahead by a point, but either man could win it in the next, or it could even be a draw. And neither skills nor courage would decide the winner—anatomy would. Frazier, the shorter man, always fought from a crouch; however, both his eyes were badly swollen. Futch, realizing that Frazier would have to straighten just to get minimal vision, shook his head sadly and told Benton to cut the gloves off. Frazier protested violently, but Futch, with an arm around Frazier's shoulders, said, "Son, there's always another day. Your eyes are too important for me not to stop this."

It was always this way with these two men. Each inevitably made the other better than he was. Once again, as George Foreman said, "Styles make fights and their styles dictated that if they fought a hundred times, it would always be a life or death thing."

In the end, it was Ali's finest hour. Some say his finest came against Foreman, and indeed, the Foreman fight was very much a part of his legend because of the long, seemingly impossible road back to the title. However, against Frazier, it was a walk through hell in which Ali was supremely tested as a fighter for the ages. Few could have made it through that fight. Who knows if another heavyweight could have survived those furious assaults on the ropes that Frazier dealt him? It could have easily ended in one of those moments. But Ali came back the stronger of the two, and won with honor.

As for Frazier, well, his story is obvious. In battered and painful seclusion in his dressing room, with the door closed, he said to Futch, Benton, and Bailey, "I was there, wasn't I? But his reach . . . that's something you can't do nothing about."

The door opened and Marvis Frazier came in. Crying, he hugged his daddy and said, "Daddy, you will always be my champ."

Frazier smiled through battered lips. "I'll take it, son."

Across the hall, Ali sat, exhausted. He turned to Gene Kilroy, and said: "Joe Frazier gave me hell. He's the greatest fighter I will ever fight."

It was, indeed, a Thrilla in Manila.

SEVEN

Is This the End of Muhammad Ali?

"[Ali] should hang it up. He's going to get hurt."
—*Teddy Brenner*

He had out-gutted Joe Frazier in the greatest heavyweight title fight ever staged. It was hardly time for another trauma. So Muhammad Ali took a deep breath and relaxed with a trilogy of soft touches. He went down to Puerto Rico and stopped a Flemish sculptor named Jean-Pierre Coopman in five rounds, after which Coopman embraced him and asked for an autograph.

Landover, Maryland, was next, as was a very talented boxer named Jimmy Young, whose best days were behind him. Here, the word *boxer* is used advisedly. Young's strength was in his ring smarts. However, nobody ever out-boxed Ali, and Young's principal offense consisted of sticking his head out of the ropes and benefitting because the referee didn't know that each instance should have been scored as a knockdown. Ali, of course, won.

Then came a vacation trip to Munich to fight a British ex-paratrooper named Richard Dunn. Ali stopped him in five rounds. The event was notable because, to save television the embarrassment of empty seats, Ali bought hundreds of tickets and gave them away to American soldiers stationed there.

However, a real fight was at hand. Three years earlier, Ken Norton had broken Ali's jaw as a 5–1 underdog. They fought a second time six months later, and Ali won in a highly questionable decision. Most writers at ringside, including me, had disagreed with the judges and given it to Norton. Once again, it was time for unfinished business.

In truth, Norton was an athlete first and foremost, who later became a great boxer. A four-sport letter winner in high school, he was so gifted he once finished first in fourteen events in a high school track meet. He was big and strong, and always seemed to move forward. However, he had an awkward fighting style, seeming to drag his right foot from behind. His stance also featured a cross-armed defense rarely seen in the sport. This latter style became a puzzle that Ali had trouble solving.

The third fight between Ali and Norton on September 28, 1976, promoted by Bob Arum and held in Yankee Stadium, was one of the last outdoor fights in the United States. On picture day, the fighters were photographed separately. Ali ran around the outfield for the television cameras, throwing punches and shouting while huge letters blazed on the big stadium scoreboard: "Is this the end of Muhammad Ali?"

The fight was set for the big stadium in the city that never sleeps. What a moment; what a venue. What could possibly go wrong?

Everything.

On that night in the Bronx, the New York Police Department did the unimaginable thing. Its union organized a strike for a new contract that day, essentially voting with its feet against the need to serve and protect.

Nobody believed it would actually happen. On the eve of the fight, Arum met with top police brass, city, and stadium officials. "We were assured," Arum recalled, "that everything would be under control." With that in mind, the Yankees opened 108 ticket kiosks for fight night.

Exactly ten whole, entire tickets were sold on that night. It was probably the worst walk-up sale in the history of the planet. Police pickets were chanting slogans, and gangs of thugs roamed the streets around the ballpark, assaulting and robbing people of their wallets and sportswriters of their typewriters. It was absolute chaos.

"Ticket holders and those who came to buy tickets got off the subway, saw what was happening, and turned around and got back on the trains," Arum said. Outside the stadium, the line of police pickets managed to achieve the impossible through its inaction. It turned acres of traffic into the world's largest carbon monoxide–tainted pretzel while it filled the street, blowing whistles, and chanting four-letter epithets at the Mayor of the City of New York.

Inside the ballpark, Mayor Abraham Beame was loudly reiterating that he needed a forceful way to punish every striking cop. The next day, I mused that if he were really serious about revenge, he should have ordered Arum to throw open the gates for all the picketers and forced them to sit through one of the worst heavyweight title fights in history. That would have been about as cruel and unusual as a punishment can get.

Ken Norton was willing, but his thoughts were more of revenge than money. Ali fought off memory, but his talent was fading. They huffed and puffed and were never in mortal danger of blowing each other down. The referee, Arthur Mercante, whose job was to keep order, got so much of it that he had to remind the fighters what it was they were supposed to be doing. He warned Ali four times for holding. Norton's corner was launching a fusillade of rhetoric, a sort of play-by-play that led me to conclude they had a hidden television set in the corner and were watching some other fight. Ali, meanwhile, kept waving to spectacularly empty seats, their absence proving that boxing fans are smarter than most people think.

Ali's biggest contribution between the second and seventh rounds was a series of scatological remarks between missed punches. Norton fought back with a series of vocal outbursts suggesting that Ali perform an anatomically impossible act. It may have been the only fight in history where two men, weighing more than 215 pounds each, fought as though sticks and stones could not break their bones but names could wallop the hell out of them.

In between shouted discussions, Norton forced the only fight that was happening and was clearly ahead. The wind off the river was a spear pointed at the few spectators' hearts. Arum admitted in retrospect, "It was a horrible fight on a horrible night. Ali seemed to have left all that he had been in the ring in Manila after the Frazierfight."

Norton was ahead going into the late rounds, and he savored the thought of revenge. But blows, however feeble, translate into points on judges' scorecards. That knowledge carried Ali, who finally began to fight a little. Rhetoric, which Norton savored, replaced his punches as anticipated vindication. He ran around the ring, sticking his tongue out, laughing at Ali, and throwing virtually no punches, and ultimately gave away the fight. Ali erased all his earlier sins in the eleventh round when he landed six consecutive right hands, making up in accuracy what he lost in impact. With each punch you could almost hear Ali think: *Fool, I'll let you be the clown. It's cold and I'm old, and if you won't take it from me, then here's a little something to remind the judges.*

In short, Ali stole the thing—and he knew it. His victory was without glory or witnesses. "Maybe it's time I quit," he told us in the post-fight press conference. He was right.

But he was also Ali. He ignored his own advice, and a world of trouble awaited him.

It began innocently enough with a desultory fifteen-round decision over Alfredo Evangelista, a Spaniard of minimal skills. Despite what he had admitted after the Norton debacle, and despite what those who did not view him as a cash cow warned against, including his former promoter, Bob Arum, and Madison Square Garden matchmaker, Teddy Brenner, Ali signed to fight Ernie Shavers on September 29, 1977.

I saw them all during that period, a roster of heavyweights who were the greatest generation of their class. And I can tell you that Shavers was the hardest single puncher in the bunch—harder than Foreman, harder than Frazier, harder than Holmes. He won 74 of 89 fights, and his 68 knockouts scared the hell out of most of his contemporaries. He could box well. The flaw that kept him from becoming a heavyweight champion in the middle of the greatest collection of heavyweights was his chin, which was suspect.

It was a fight Ali should have run from in his declining years. But Ali was Ali. Tell him he shouldn't and he damned well would. It was Ali's view that the heavy-footed Shavers, who had a reputation for fading in the late rounds, was made for him. The pre-fight hours, therefore, were marked with Muhammad's usual show biz performance.

"His head is shaved," Ali proclaimed. "He looks funny. Look at it. I officially nickname him 'the Acorn.'"

In the second round, all the fun and games went out the window. Shavers hit with a tremendous overhand right and staggered Ali. Ali tried to clown his way through the round, but he moved on noticeably wobbly legs. Ali gathered himself, survived, and went on to build up points. In the thirteenth Shavers bombarded him and stunned him again, owning the ring geography. When the bell rang for the fifteenth round, Ali was in deep trouble.

Ultimately, Ali reached down and turned it around, hammering Shavers at the finish to win a unanimous decision. However, he later told me, "I think I might have been out on my feet for a while."

The reaction was immediate. Teddy Brenner, the Garden's matchmaker, insisted that Shavers should have gotten the decision. "[Ali] should hang it up," he said. "He's going to get hurt." But who could he fight now that time had eroded his skills?

Back when Arum and King were promoting Ali–Frazier III in Manila, a guy from Philadelphia had attached himself to Arum. The common thread that had brought him to Arum was Frazier. Butch Lewis, whose father owned a car dealership, had sold Frazier a motorcycle. He began to hang around with the promoter in Manila, and after the fight, Arum hired him.

The United States sent more boxing talent to the 1976 Olympic Games than it had ever before sent anywhere. These were the games of Leon and Michael Spinks, Sugar Ray Leonard, Howard Davis, and John Tate, just to name the headliners. Arum, always on the hunt for new fighters with star potential, planned to attend, and it occurred to him that a smooth talker like Lewis, with his youth and ability to play the race card on his side, just might be an asset in dealing with a couple of potential signees. Before they left for Montreal, Arum assigned Lewis the task of convincing the Spinks brothers to join their side.

Michael Spinks was by far the better, although smaller, fighter. Leon Spinks was the light heavyweight growing toward heavyweight dimensions; however, he was seriously irresponsible and addicted to alcohol. It helped somewhat that Michael, a middleweight with genuine talent, put his career on hold to watch out for Leon. As he told me, "I never went to college, but I can read, write, and add numbers, so I am determined to look after him." As things developed, Leon might never have made any progress without Michael's support.

Leon's personal history clearly indicated that. The Spinks family lived in St. Louis's infamous Pruitt-Igoe Homes, a public housing development so crime-infested and so out of control that the government finally demolished it. "He was always picked on by the bullies," Michael told me. "I protected him. I had to do his fighting for him."

As a teenager, frightened and undisciplined, Leon ran away from home and moved into the Railroad YMCA and Gym Hotel. Mitt Barnes, a St. Louis teamsters union organizer, gave him money and trained him as an amateur until he went into the Marines. It was understood between the two that, when he turned professional, Mitt would be the manager and receive a third of his earnings.

However, the success of the two brothers in the 1976 Olympics changed all of that. At Arum's behest, Butch Lewis gained both brothers' confidence. Leon was now living in Philadelphia (at Butch's suggestion) and being trained by a local handler of note named Sam Solomon. Almost immediately, Leon was caught in the middle of a tug-of-war between Lewis and Barnes. As Lewis took more and more control over Spinks, Barnes would later sue Top Rank, a boxing promotion company, and win his fair share of both Spinks–Ali fights.

But before Leon reached Ali, he rode crest of his Olympic publicity, staggering forward. He won six straight fights and got a draw in bouts against incredibly mediocre competition. After a horrible performance in beating Bob Smith (whose record was just 7–7–1), Arum had reason to worry when he received a phone call that night from Barry Frank, the vice president of CBS Sports, which had televised the fight. "I want you here first thing tomorrow morning," Frank said.

At first, Arum was convinced that CBS was angry and that the overall plan was in jeopardy. "But when I got there," Arum said, "Frank and Neal Pilson, the president of the sports division, came rushing into the lobby and hugged me. They're yelling, 'We love you.' I couldn't believe it, but the fight had drawn a humongous viewer rating."

They were rolling toward the easy fight Ali was requesting. Inexplicably, two of Spinks's six opponents failed to show. In England, a fellow named Eddie Fenton was suddenly replaced by Peter Freeman (alleged to have a 13–8 record). Freeman was counted out in the first round. In Canada, George Jerome never showed up on fight night, and Bruce Scott (alleged to have a 10–37–1 record) was obligingly counted out in the third. Then, Spinks fought a nightmarish draw with Scott LeDoux and finally decisioned Alfio Righetti in a fight best remembered for Lewis racing up and down the first row at ringside, shouting as Spinks put on a desultory performance, "Dammit, Leon, you gotta do something. You are blowing this fight. You are on your way back to the ghetto."

Looking at that record, you might wonder why Leon Spinks might even be considered among the greats. I was at both of his title fights with Ali, and I still wonder how a semi-sober kid barely out of the amateurs managed to spend more than two hundred days as the king of the heavyweight hill.

Certainly, Ali never expected it. When he found out he was to fight Spinks, he was mortified. "Don't expect me to promote this," he said. "I ain't talking to no reporters. I'm embarrassed." How can you have an Ali fight without Ali's headline-grabbing voice? Irving Rudd, a brilliant publicist in Top Rank, came up with the perfect answer. "He will take a vow of religious silence not to be broken until fight week."

Satisfied, Ali returned to the 5th Street Gym in Miami Beach and barred reporters from the building. The only reason he spoke to me was because Kilroy prevailed upon him to do so. I have had far more meaningful interviews in my time. Sitting on the passenger side of his car, he rolled down the window and said things like, "How are you? How is the family? I expect to win. Goodbye."

Even for Ali, his projected over-confidence was overwhelming. It didn't suffer any a few days before the fight when, as he was on his way out of the hotel at 6 a.m. to run, he met a drunken Spinks returning from a night out.

"Ridiculous," Ali said. "I don't need to do nothin'. I'm goin' to the coffee shop."

And he did.

Meanwhile, a strange drama was secretly happening in, of all places, Leon Spinks's bathroom. Ironically, it was the best boxing move Butch Lewis ever made. Lewis had secretly hired George Benton, one of the greatest Philadelphia boxers of all, who was born to train fighters. His mastery of an opponent's weakness was terrific, and Eddie Futch and Joe Frazier had employed it for the Thrilla in Manila. Spinks had no faith in his trainer Solomon, but Lewis could not undermine Solomon because he was ever-present at Spinks's side. So, he brought Benton in with secret sessions in Spinks's bathroom.

On February 15, 1978 when Spinks and Ali met in the ring, Spinks pulled off the upset of the century (or, more accurately, Ali snatched defeat out of the jaws of victory). I was in the hotel coffee shop at 3 a.m. when I found George Benton eating a sandwich at the counter. He explained to me how they did it.

"The people around Leon didn't want me . . . not Sam [Solomon], and not Michael [Spinks's brother], who felt that his closeness with his brother was threatened. So, we would hide in [Leon's] bathroom. Sometimes we would talk, and sometimes I would show him things.

"I showed him how to bob and weave, which he had never learned. We acted it out over and over. And then I showed him the punch that I believed could win this fight: the uppercut. In certain situations, Ali was vulnerable to it. We weren't going to knock him out; we couldn't if we tried. But then, we didn't have to do that. All we had to do was pressure him, and make Leon's head a moving target with feints. I didn't believe Ali was in shape for a fifteen-rounder.

"Honestly, Ali was just a shadow of the great fighter we all knew. He had been a slipper of punches—fast hand speed, fast foot speed—but age takes that away. I believed if Leon pressured him . . . came in behind a jab . . . did those things, he would win.

"So we did it. But damned if I will put up with the same mess if he wants me back."

Never had a challenger gone to battle with a better blueprint.

If this was indeed the end of Muhammad Ali, then I wondered what the beginning of that end was. I believe it happened in the tenth round. Ali had begun to punch his way back into a fight he was losing. Midway through, he caught Spinks on the ropes and landed a thunderous left hook that rocked his head back against the top strand. A right cross landed. Another hook and another right pinned Spinks against the ropes. Then, time ticked away from his aging legs. He had a little more than a minute left to finish the job, and he couldn't. Ali didn't need the announcement at the end. He knew he had handed it to Spinks more than Spinks had taken it away from him.

At 1 a.m. in Vegas, I stood in that empty ring and did a stand-up for a TV station in New York. There were discarded hand wraps on the floor, and one stool still in the ring. How many rings had I seen Ali in? I didn't need a script. I remember saying that, if this was the end of Ali, it was at the wrong time in the wrong place. I had seen him fight with a broken hand. I had seen him fight with a broken jaw. I had seen him win in the fiery furnace that was Manila, when he and Joe Frazier made each other better than they actually were. Now I had seen him lose it all decisively to a rank amateur.

However, he was still Muhammad Ali. This was boxing, where things are rarely what they seem to be, and the shock of such a defeat was nothing compared to the unexpected chaos that would soon follow. It would involve the only man ever to win the title by diploma and immediately lose it. It would involve the return of Muhammad Ali in the land of Marie Laveau. It would involve the end of Leon Spinks. And even with all that, some of the best of this remarkable era was yet to come.

Genuine boxing fans understood that, from an artistic standpoint, the Ali–Spinks rematch was not going to be a mega-fight, not as long as Ali hadn't disintegrated to the point where even Spinks's limited skills would be too much. But as H. L. Mencken, the brilliant Baltimore newspaper columnist, once said, "Nobody ever went broke by underestimating the taste of the American public."

The intense split passions of the American public when it came to Ali did, indeed, turn the money to be made from the event worthy of that of a mega fight. That was true even though it should have been clear that Spinks still remained, in truth, a rank amateur.

The venue would be New Orleans.

It was a city with a serious boxing history. In 1892, John L. Sullivan was undefeated and fought Gentleman Jim Corbett in front of ten thousand spectators at the Olympic Club in New Orleans. Corbett gave him a one-sided boxing lesson and knocked him out in the twenty-first round. Further history of the sport can be found by the levee on River Road in nearby Kenner, where a statue marks the spot an Englishman named Jem Mace won the first world championship by beating his countryman Tom Allen in 1870.

For a full century, New Orleans became a town where boxing thrived because the locals understood it. Neighborhood kids became city-wide heroes—fighters like Bernard and Maxie Docusen and champions Ralph Dupas and Willie Pastrano. Regular fight cards at places like the Municipal Auditorium and the Rivergate on Canal Street were a major attraction.

Now there was the New Orleans Superdome, the perfect stage just waiting for Muhammad Ali. He knew the end was near. He knew how he wanted to handle it. He trained ferociously. He cut down on distractions. He was determined to take Leon Spinks to school, to a place he had never been, to a place that would completely befuddle him.

Ironically, Ali received serious and unanticipated help from, of all places, Leon Spinks's own people. It began when an intramural feud between the two camps boiled over during an ad hoc meeting at the Hilton Hotel a week before the fight.

Sam Solomon, the trainer of record, and Michael Spinks, Leon's brother, were there. Art Reddon, the Marine sergeant who had trained Spinks at Camp Lejeune, was there. Butch Lewis, who had captured Spinks's loyalty, was there. However, Spinks himself, who desperately needed the counsel and reassurance Benton had given him before and during the first fight in Las Vegas, was not.

Each, for reasons of his own, agreed that he did not welcome a return of George Benton to the camp. The one exception was Lewis, who understood that Benton, whose sights were set on becoming Spinks's only man, had effectively won the last fight for Spinks.

Lewis won the argument, and Benton arrived the next day, a Wednesday. The fight was on Saturday. It was far too little and way too late.

Five minutes before Team Spinks left for the arena on fight night, Solomon called Benton aside and revealed the worst corner plan in the history of heavyweight championship boxing. He explained that Michael Spinks, Art Reddon, Butch Lewis's brother, Nelson, and George Benton would alternate in the corner as the third man. He and the cut man, Pop Bailey, would work each round.

"The next day," Benton told me, "There were ten guys in the corner, so what can you do. This kid needed help badly, and they expect me to go up and down like a damned yo-yo. They had so many guys jumping in and out of the corner the commissioner jumped into the ring and threatened to fine them. So, during the seventh round I said, 'What the hell am I doing here?' and I walked . . . right out of the ring . . . right out of the damned building . . . the longest walk of my life—but I did the right thing."

Benton did not underestimate how much help Spinks needed. That night, Ali did exactly what he said he'd do. He did it with the jab. He did it to the face of a fighter with whom he had an eleven-year age gap. He did it with the marvelous pivot that, each time, brought him off the ropes with his back to the center of the ring where he predicted it would be.

Ali owned the center of the ring, staying off the ropes and setting a pattern that would be maintained. His jab took him where he wanted to go. He would follow it with a slip on the right and a left hook or a slip to the left and a right hand. Manila was grittier, Zaire was more dramatic—but this was textbook boxing. This was the master wraith, slipping and sticking, locking, then socking.

Spinks didn't have a chance. The left hand that had rattled and defeated Ali in Vegas seemed to be encased in feathers. Ali made that happen by owning the distance between him and Spinks, stretching himself to where he, with his long reach, could pop jabs in Spinks's face. It also forced Spinks to lunge to reach him, with each lunge putting Spinks more off-balance. And whenever he got close enough, Ali was more than willing to take three hits in order to land one. While Spinks's punches had no power, Ali's one hit always rocked the fading champion. It was as though Spinks had abandoned every weapon he had taken into the first fight.

By the seventh round, it was clear that Spinks was in a fight where he had no answers to the hammering Ali was administering. Ali seemed to smile, knowing what would happen next. In the eighth, he fired two stiff left jabs and finished with a ferocious right hand. The round ended as Spinks tried to clutch Ali to halt the onslaught. At the bell, the arena erupted in a thunderous sound that grew to a crescendo, shaking the building to its very core. Ali walked back to his corner, both arms raised in salute. In that instant, the hope with which he had entered the ring morphed into a conviction. He knew now how to win it—and how to do it with style.

Across the ring, Michael Spinks was leaning in and whispering to his brother. Sam Solomon was pleading. And Muhammad Ali, catching a photographer's eye, winked. I recalled something he had told me that summer.

"It got to be different this time, man. Time is wiping me out as a boxer. I'd be a fool not to know that. I want this one. It could be the last one."

It was that fear that drove him to reach back and fight off memory, and he won it by light years. If this would be his last dance, then he had autographed it in neon lights. It was time to pay off the orchestra, put away the yearbook, and get off stage.

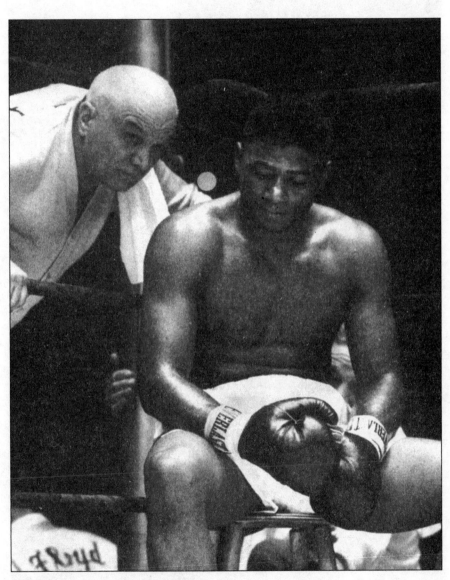

Cus D'Amato and Floyd Patterson in the corner.

Ali–Jones, March 13, 1963.
Photo credit: Boxing Hall of Fame of Las Vegas

Ali–Cooper, June 18, 1965.
Photo credit: Boxing Hall of Fame of Las Vegas

Frazier–Ali I, March 8, 1971.
Photo credit: Boxing Hall of Fame of Las Vegas

Ali–Foreman, October 30, 1974.

Muhammad Ali knocks down George Foreman, October 30, 1974.

Ali–Foreman knockdown, October 30, 1974.
Photo credit: Boxing Hall of Fame of Las Vegas

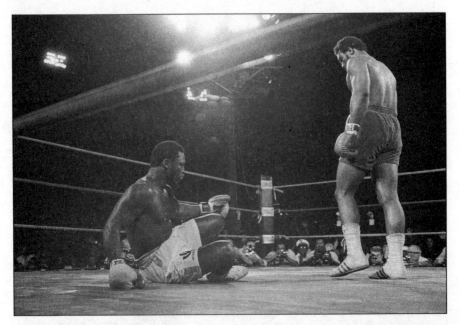

Foreman–Frazier I, January 22, 1973.

Young–Foreman, March 17, 1977.

Holmes–Norton, June 9, 1978.
Photo credit: Boxing Hall of Fame of Las Vegas

Ali–Spinks II, September 15, 1978.
Photo credit: Boxing Hall of Fame of Las Vegas

Holmes–Spinks II, April 19, 1986.
Photo credit: Boxing Hall of Fame of Las Vegas

Cus D'Amato and Mike Tyson.
Photo credit: Boxing Hall of Fame of Las Vegas

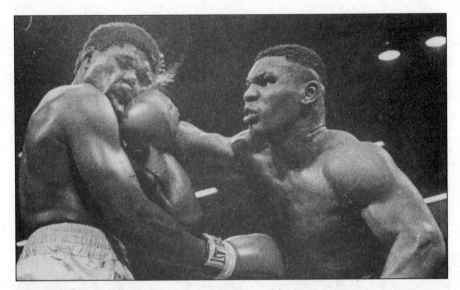

Tyson–Tillis, May 3, 1986.
Photo credit: Boxing Hall of Fame of Las Vegas

Tyson–Green, May 20, 1986.
Photo credit: Boxing Hall of Fame of Las Vegas

Tyson–Thomas, May 30, 1987.
Photo credit: Boxing Hall of Fame of Las Vegas

A young Jerry Izenberg at ringside in Caesars Palace.

Muhammad Ali and Jerry Izenberg look at family pictures in a limo.
From the private collection of Jerry Izenberg

Jerry Izenberg punches Muhammad Ali.
From the private collection of Jerry Izenberg

Jerry Izenberg and Joe Frazier.
Photo credit: Gene Kilroy

Jerry Izenberg interviews Leon Spinks before Ali–Spinks, February 15, 1978.
From the private collection of Jerry Izenberg

Jerry Izenberg and referee Joe Cortez show off their rings in the lobby of the International Boxing Hall of Fame.
Photo credit: International Boxing Hall of Fame, Inc.

EIGHT

The Champion Who Became a Trivia Question

"I broke Ali's jaw. They took away the decision the second time, but I know I can beat Holmes. I deserve this chance."

—*Ken Norton*

"It wasn't trainers that really taught me. I learned from those three guys—Shavers, Frazier, and Ali. I learned when I was a sparring partner. I learned not to get hit, I learned to hit back, and I learned my way around the ring. They were my teachers. I never learned a great deal from my trainers."

—*Larry Holmes*

Once again, boxing returned to normalcy, which is to say nothing made sense. Ali, who had announced his long overdue retirement after decisively winning Ali–Spinks II, was the catalyst. His parting shot only added to the frenetic career that preceded it. All along, he had made it clear that he would never be anybody's puppet, particularly when it came to somebody telling him who, what, when, and where he should fight.

Just before Ali's first fight with Leon Spinks in February 1978, Bob Arum had gone to Mexico City to calm the fears of José Sulaimáns. The head of the World Boxing Council (WBC) was in a panic. Ali had signed to fight Spinks for the title against Sulaimán's wishes, possibly interfering with Sulaimán's chance to scoop up future thousands in sanctioning fees, leaving him empty-handed down the line. Sulaimán had wanted the champion to fight the winner of a proposed Norton–Young eliminator. When Arum convinced Sulaimán that Ali would do just that, but only after the Spinks fight, Sulaimán agreed not to strip Ali of the WBC title on the condition that both agree to the terms, so he was covered no matter who won.

On November 5, 1977, Ken Norton fought Jimmy Young at Caesars Palace in Las Vegas in an interesting match-up of styles. Norton was a banger, always moving forward, disdaining the beauty of the jab in favor of the crushing hammer of power punches. Young had a fair amount of power, but it was his skill as a master boxer that made him a difficult opponent.

Norton won a highly controversial split decision. Two of the three judges combined to score an incredible eleven even rounds. Only a panel of myopic bats could have turned in scores like that. On my scorecard, Young had won by two rounds. The referee, Sonny Padilla, the same man who had refereed Ali–Frazier III, said that if he had had a vote (the referee does not score), his scorecard would have been the same as mine.

Sulaimán was ecstatic. With Arum's promise of a title fight with Norton in his pocket he faced the future with confidence—for a few months or so until. Ali proceeded to lose his fight with Spinks. Suddenly, both Ali and Spinks weren't thinking about Sulaimán and the agreement; they were thinking instead about the incredible financial bonanza they could share if they fought a rematch. Sulaimán was cooked as soon as the referee raised Spinks's hand. The morning after, Spinks sat in his suite on the nineteenth floor of the Las Vegas Hilton and told a few of us that he would be glad to give Ali a rematch. When I said, "But didn't you agree to fight Norton [who had beaten Young] if you won?" He replied, "Ask my lawyer."

One hour later and ten floors higher, Ali held court in his own suite. "Do you think [Spinks] should fight you next?" I asked. "He's the champion," Ali responded. "The champion is the person who decides who he should fight—not some commissioner." With the amount of money the Ali–Spinks rematch would earn, Arum would have counseled him to drink muddy water and sleep in a hollow log before he passed up an opportunity like that. Sulaimán was left with an empty promise. The WBC had nothing to counter with once the rematch was signed. Enraged, Sulaimán immediately stripped Spinks of his new title and rushed to declare Norton the WBC champion.

Ali and Spinks were soon New Orleans–bound for the rematch that Ali would easily win, after which he would retire. Sulaimán was left with the taste of ashes and a paper champion. Ken Norton appeared to be back where he started. He had broken Ali's jaw once, lost two controversial decisions after that, and still not won a title in the ring. If wishes were horses, he probably would have gotten hoof and mouth disease.

Suddenly, both Norton and Sulaimán shared ownership of a championship with neither legitimacy nor challenger. Norton, a champion who had never won a title fight, had turned into a trivia question. With Norton thus anointed, they had half a title fight. And if Norton, with all his near misses, was the victim of bad luck, Larry Holmes, the man Norton would finally fight in defense of his paper title, seemed to have no luck at all.

Larry Holmes came out of a public housing project in Easton, Pennsylvania, dropped out of elementary school in the seventh grade to help support his mother and his siblings, and didn't set foot in a boxing gym until he was nineteen. After a brief amateur career, he turned pro. During those early years, he was a hero in Easton and a phantom in pretty much the rest of the world.

Eight of his first ten fights were held in the Catholic Youth Center in Scranton, Pennsylvania. He won all ten. A fellow named Ernie Butler was his first manager and trainer, and it was Butler who took him to Muhammad Ali's training camp and offered his services as a sparring partner.

Holmes remained undefeated and unnoticed during these years when he would also spar fairly regularly with Ali, Frazier, and Ernie Shavers. "It wasn't trainers that really taught me," he told me. "I learned from those three guys. I learned not to get hit, I learned to hit back, and I learned my way around the ring. They were my teachers. I never learned a great deal from my trainers."

Don King eventually took over from Butler; however, he was not overly enthusiastic about his new signee. After all, he was promoting Ali's fights at the time. From a reputation point of view, Holmes was still little more than the king of Scranton's Catholic Youth Center.

It was halfway around the world, in the Philippines of all places, that Larry Holmes finally got himself noticed—on the undercard of Ali–Frazier III in 1975. It was there that he first fought a name opponent, conquering any doubts or fears for the future he may have had.

Holmes was scheduled for a ten-rounder against Rodney Bobick, the brother of Olympic heavyweight Duane Bobick, who had won his spot in the Games by beating Holmes, then an amateur, in the Olympic Trials. Larry was 16–0 and Rodney was 34–5 going into the fight.

Rodney Bobick was not the only problem Holmes faced. Duane Bobick was under contract with Joe Frazier to manage him, and Angelo Dundee, Ali's trainer, trained Rodney. Because of this, neither Frazier's nor Ali's camp would let Holmes use their equipment or sparring partners. Additionally, Don King, Holmes's promoter, made no effort to help. In an act of desperation, Holmes recruited Jerry Lisker, a former college-boxer-turned-sportswriter, to help him. Together, they ran during the mornings and shadow boxed in the hotel's corridor.

None of Holmes's snubs had an impact on fight night, as a worldwide television audience watched Holmes for the first time in his career. He set the pace with a masterful jab, coming in behind it with either straight right hands or right uppercuts, and stopping Bobick at 2:47 of the sixth round.

Ken Norton provided the color commentary on television. Afterward, when asked if he would be fighting Holmes one day, he prophetically responded, "I'd rather get him now than later." It was an off-hand comment that, for Norton, might as well have been the Ghost of Christmas Yet to Come. Three years later, on June 9, 1978, Larry Holmes became the opponent for Norton's first (and only) defense of José Sulaimán's ersatz championship at Caesars Palace in Las Vegas. He had earned that right three months earlier, with a surprisingly easy decision triumph over the same Earnie Shavers, who once had Ali almost out on his feet.

The Monday preceding the fight, all hell broke loose. Holmes was talking with the media in his dressing room when the Norton camp charged in, demanding he leave the arena before Norton began his own workout. Holmes refused; four-letter words and gestures designed to mean more four-letter words took over. Then, Holmes pushed Norton, later explaining, "He was gonna shove me, so I shoved first."

A few days prior, promoter Don King had announced that he was inviting a group no smaller than the entire population of Reno to attend what he proudly called "the first hustlers ball"—a party he effectively threw around himself. The guests started to trickle in early that morning, appropriately attired in what urbanites refer to as "the wardrobe of the night people." By noon, the lobby looked like a subway platform in Oz. It was just another occasion that demonstrated King's lack of interest in helping Holmes, especially in the moments where he needed it the most.

A day before, in the locked sports pavilion in fortunate isolation, Holmes was sparring with a guy named Luis Rodriguez when he raised his left arm to block a looping right hand and took the blow on his biceps. He felt a tear inside the muscle, and it delivered an agonizing pain from his eyebrows to his ankles. He was taken out of there as quickly as possible, but nobody had to tell him that it was bad. The bicep was torn.

From the moment Larry Holmes tore that biceps, his hopes, his career, and all those miles of lonely roadwork he had run in Easton alongside the juncture of the Lehigh and Delaware Rivers were left in the healing hands of Dr. Keith Kleven. Holmes found himself at a critical moment when the fight walked a fine line between cancellation and salvation—all on the recommendation of the doctor. The future of the fight was in his hands. Covered by a secret cone of silence, Kleven, who ran the physical therapy department at Desert Pines Hospital, worked every afternoon with Holmes. It is possible that even Don King did not know what had happened. The fight was just five days away.

Kleven used a machine called a high galvanic stimulator, which held the electronic key to reducing the swelling and restoring blood flow.

"He's gonna fight," Richie Giachetti, his trainer, insisted.

"Maybe," Kleven replied.

"He's my fighter," Giachetti said.

"He's my patient," Kleven said. "He needs a healthy triceps to jab. I can't decide right away."

"He's fightin'," Giachetti said.

"We'll see," Kleven replied.

On the morning of the fight, twenty minutes before the weigh-in, Kleven sat alone with Holmes and told him, "We did all we can do. You can fight if you protect yourself. You can jab [the very life-blood of Holmes's arsenal], but you have to take your time with what you do and be careful. If you get hit on that biceps, I can guarantee nothing after that."

That warning came to fruition after the first six rounds, during which Holmes's jab seemed to be the great eraser when measured against Norton's attempts to overwhelm him with sheer power. If this would be the pattern of the fight, it was clear Holmes would win with his master boxing lesson. However, the next round changed everything. Ken Norton unleashed a looping right hand that Holmes moved to block with his left arm. The punch landed flush on the torn muscle. Norton had no idea about the injury beforehand, but he immediately sensed that the challenger had suddenly turned cautious. During another heated exchange involving Holmes's right hand, he felt a new burst of pain—a re-aggravated old injury. Medically, a doctor might have pronounced that he had just lost the effectiveness of both hands.

"I knew I had the style to beat Norton because the jab would back him up," Holmes told me years later. "But after he hit my left arm, I had to use it carefully and less often. He scored points. But when we got deep into the fight, I said the hell with it. I had come too far—pain or no pain."

For once, my scorecard was the same as the three judges'. The four of us had it dead even going into round fifteen. So did everyone in both corners. When the bell rang, it set in motion what I believe to be the greatest single final round in the history of the modern heavyweights. "It hurt," Holmes said, "but I felt like Keith had given me a way in, and I was going to take it."

At the bell, Freddie Brown, the old veteran cornerman, dumped a ton of water on Holmes's head and yelled at him, "Stay loose, stay loose." Both fighters came back out on wobbly legs.

The temperature in the ring was surely a hundred degrees under the television lights. Here came Norton, willing himself forward with that strange cross-handed guard of his. Holmes feinted with the jab, and Norton walloped him with one left hook and then another, and then a right to the head. Holmes's mouth was awash in blood. With each punch Norton threw he nearly collapsed himself, and with each punch that landed Holmes nearly collapsed. For much of the round, Norton banged out a slow, painful dirge of a margin. He seemed to be winning.

"I wasn't going to get another chance unless I got it done right there," Holmes explained later. "What else went through your mind?" I asked. "I remember thinking I can't let my body betray me now. I remember thinking, hell with it, and I started to throw the jab the way I needed to throw it."

That wasn't all he threw. In the final third of the fifteenth round, his right hand caught Norton flush on the chin and staggered him. Now Holmes was all over him. Norton backed off, his legs buckling, and when he tried to fight back the power was already gone.

The scorecards added up to a split decision. It was decided by that final round. Two judges saw it for Holmes, one for Norton. The loser had never been more courageous, and the winner never more heroic.

Two years later, Mike Weaver decisioned Gerrie Coetzee in South Africa to win the WBA championship. The heavyweight title would remain splintered until 1988, when Mike Tyson would destroy Michael Spinks. But that's another story that would be a long time in the making.

Now, the story was all Larry Holmes, underrated and barely known but getting a hell of a lot better each time out. Back in November of 1977, he was matched in a ten-rounder against a journeyman heavyweight named Ibar "the Sailor" Arrington, whom he would stop in the final round. The day before that fight, we were walking toward a bank of elevators in Caesars Palace when a woman, basing her own conclusion off Larry's six-three-foot height, stopped us. "Excuse me. Which basketball team do you play for? My husband and I would like to buy tickets for the game."

After she left, Holmes turned to me and said, "I never lost a fight. I'm 25–0. What the hell I got to do to get them to know who I am?"

Well, this is who I believed he was: the man who possessed one of the three best heavyweight jabs among the moderns, including Sonny Liston and Joe Louis; the man with an absolutely devastating uppercut that his corner named "Big Jack" after the late, great Jack Johnson; and, finally, the man who never really got the credit due him (along with Joe Frazier) because of the long shadow cast by the legend of Muhammad Ali.

Make no mistake about it: when Holmes and Ali finally signed to fight each other in the twilight of Ali's career, it hurled Holmes into a no-win situation. Ali was now a shadow of the man who dominated the heavyweights. If Holmes won, he would have beaten a washed up superstar. If he lost, well, you can only imagine how history would have viewed Larry.

No fight ever flew in the face of logic like the leadup to Ali–Holmes, set on October 2, 1980. Mindful of Ali's strange grip on the minds and hearts of so many, Caesars Palace took one of its parking lots and watered it with money. For $750,000, a twenty-four-thousand-seat tinker toy stadium bloomed on the Strip. The plans called for a stadium that could last a thousand years or fifteen rounds—whichever came first.

On the day he arrived in Vegas, Holmes held an impromptu press conference, during which he told us, "[Ali] was a great athlete, but now he is stepping out of his time and into mine. He doesn't belong here. He tells people he will turn back the clock of time. But he can't. All the people who yell 'Ali . . . Ali' can't help him. His corner can't fight for him. He's gotta fight and I gotta fight.

"It's as simple as that."

I was sitting in the living room of Holmes's suite, where a small hand-lettered sign was pasted on the large mirror. It read: "My daughter, my wife, my family, and my house." It was the well-ordered list of a man who constantly reminded himself of his priorities. Evidence of Holmes's dedication came from a high chair across the room where his daughter, Larie Kandy Holmes, reaching down from her mother's arm, knocked over a glass of orange juice and displayed a single tooth as she crooned, "Dada . . . Dada . . . Dada."

Holmes laughed and said to her, "As many times as you say it, that's how many rounds I'll let him last." Then, for my benefit, he added, "Look at that sign. It tells you why I fight. I never wanted this fight. If I win—and I will—they will say I beat an old man. If he wins—and he won't—they'll say I'm a bum.

"Now I'm faced with having to do something I never intended to do. I'm going to have to knock his head off and that doesn't give me a lot of joy. But he ain't worried about my family. He wouldn't feel sorry for me. So I'll just go out and do what I got to do."

Later, as nighttime chased the dawn's early light from Room 31 where Ali passed the countdown hours, time was noticeably absent. There was only space, and, as always, Ali dominated it. He patted what appeared to be a surprisingly hard stomach. "Look at me. I can't let cake conquer me. I can't let ice cream conquer me. I know my body. I have studied under two doctors and many scientists."

Then he jumped to his feet and shadow boxed, throwing punches at a furious rate. It was, of course, play acting—a traditional greeting from an old vaudeville star returning to the stage for the last time.

"Pressure," he said, "That's on him—not me. For him, this is all new. That's his first problem. His second is when I win the first round. Now he got to win two to get ahead of me. I'll hit him pop . . . pop . . . pop . . . and then I'll knock him out. Look at this."

He ripped his shirt off and flexed his muscles. It was eerie. He had lost so much weight he looked the way he did when he stopped Sonny Liston the very first time sixteen years ago. What I did not know at the time was how he lost the weight. It turned out to be worse than I could have ever guessed. Doctors had given him serious doses of diuretics.

Ali laughed. "I'm like a kamikaze pilot pointed at a boat or a plane." I did not have the nerve to tell him what happens to kamikaze pilots—even when they win the war.

A huge sign in front of Caesars Palace read, ALI VS HOLMES, and then in smaller letters, SINATRA IN THE SHOW ROOM. Only Muhammad Ali could make a second banana out of the chairman of the board.

Strangely, as the hours rushed toward the opening bell, an incredible thing happened. The odds on Holmes began to drop to 6–5. In two casinos, they actually fell to even money. It was a first in the history of sports book betting in Sin City, because the bartenders, cab drivers, the men's room attendants, valet parkers, chambermaids, bell men, bus boys, and waitresses sent in fifty-dollar or hundred-dollar bets on the man who had been their hero for so long—Muhammad Ali.

They bet with their hearts. The wise guys, on the other hand, bet with their heads. This ain't the movies—the wise guys won.

Holmes came to do a job, and he did it. By the end of the first round, the road map had been chiseled in head-snapping jabs and thunderous hooks. Even so, the worst for his opponent, the legendary boxing icon, was yet to come.

Ali's jab and footwork had always been his miracle workers. On this night, however, the only jab in the ring belonged to Holmes. As for footwork, Ali moved as though he were trying to cross a great sand desert wearing ice skates. In short, he came to war without weapons and without a chance.

The blueprint for Holmes's victory could not be reversed. It was as painful as it was effective. Twice, Holmes shook his head after the bell as he returned to his corner. He did not relish what was happening. By the end of the second round, Ali's right eye was puffy and discolored. Just before he went out for the fourth, Angelo Dundee, Ali's chief second, screamed, "Dammit. Don't be stubborn." Ali walked out with no defense and absorbed two quick, hard jabs. An overhand right to the belly and two more jabs to the face.

Ali threw one punch, one pitiful overhand right that landed weakly on Holmes's chin and that didn't have enough power to make him blink. At the start of the fifth, Drew Brown, the Ali camp cheerleader, was leaning on the ropes, screaming, "Foul him . . . foul him." It had come to that.

By the end of the sixth, Ali's head rang from three devastating hooks. Blood trickled from his nose. His face was grotesquely swollen. It was enough for referee Richard Greene to end it, though he didn't. Round nine, the round in which Ali had predicted he would stop Holmes, was worse. He spent most of it with his back to the ropes, with Holmes between him and the center of the ring. Holmes delivered his best right hand of the fight, clearly hurting Ali. It was followed by another straight right hand and a right uppercut so vicious Ali's body quivered.

As two left hands slammed into Ali's kidney, the crowd began a strange chant of, "Ali . . . Ali . . . Ali." What they should have chanted was, "Stop it . . . stop it . . . stop it." Just before the start of round eleven, somebody did. It didn't come from Richard Greene or Angelo Dundee (although he said he did), but rather from someone sitting five rows back—Ali's long-time manager, Herbert Muhammad. He sent word to the corner and had his messenger say there was no room for debate.

The fight ended. Holmes shouldered his way across the ring and embraced the fallen champion. Richie Giachetti, Holmes's trainer, came up behind Ali and said, "You'll always be a champion."

With swollen lips and eyes, Ali shook his head. "I underestimated the mother . . . they told me he . . . he . . . it doesn't matter what they told me. I'm tellin' you he was so good . . ."

"When you fight a friend," Holmes said later that night, "you do what you got to do, but there's no joy in it. He was the one who gave me my chance when I first showed up in his camp to spar. I got a black eye that day, and Kilroy offered to put a steak on it, but I said, 'Hell no.' I got this from Ali. I want everyone in Easton to see it. He will always be a champion."

The casino was packed with the usual suspects. On that night, the tables' money-drop at Caesars would set a house record. At about 3:30 a.m., I was in the men's room where an elderly African American attendant was handing out towels. As I took mine, I asked if he had bet on the fight.

"Yes, I did."

"On whom did you bet?"

He shook his head and smiled. "Come on, you gotta know, mister. I bet on the man who first gave me my dignity—Muhammad Ali."

It wasn't an epitaph. It was a eulogy.

NINE

When Larry Met Gerry: And the Race Card Died

"There will be America, apple pie, Wheaties, and Gerry Cooney."

—*Dennis Rappaport*

From the night Larry Holmes out-gutted Ken Norton in that spectacular and brutal fifteenth round, he was a man on a mission. Just as Joe Frazier had, he felt stifled by the shadow of Muhammad Ali. He had paid his dues, but few people (especially sports writers) believed he was as good as he knew he was. After Norton, he won ten straight fights, nine of them by knockout.

During the heart of that streak, the unthinkable happened. He caught an overhand right flush on the chin from the hardest one-punch heavyweight I ever saw, Earnie Shavers, who was coming off a first-round knockout of the same Ken Norton from whom Holmes had won the title. For an instant, Holmes was on his back, completely motionless.

Holmes had easily beaten Shavers the first time they met and seemed to be on his way to an easy victory in the rematch, but that single punch almost cost him the title. After dominating Shavers in the first six rounds, Holmes was knocked down in the seventh by a right hand so ferocious I could hear the punch at ringside. I discussed that punch with some of my colleagues later that night, and all of us agreed we had doubted he could survive it. But he did and came back up in the eighth round, proving he was every bit worthy of being a champion. Holmes regained control of the fight and finished it in the eleventh, dealing Shavers a closed right eye and a trickle of blood over his left eyebrow. Holmes's performance forever laid to rest the charges against him that he lacked heart or stamina.

Who out there could possibly prevail against those qualities?

Huntington, New York, was the site of a blue-collar community on a stretch of carbon copy towns that New Yorkers called "out on the island." Gerry Cooney was raised in the last house on Holland Street, a red Cape Cod with fir trees in front and a chain-link fence around it. It was a neighborhood light years away from the projects in Easton, Pennsylvania, where Larry Holmes had spent his formative years, or, for that matter, the kind of neighborhoods that traditionally produced heavyweight champions.

Cooney's father, Tony, was a former merchant marine in World War II who worked construction jobs all over Greater New York. Tony and Eileen Cooney raised four sons and two daughters. Tony was a tough and occasionally vicious disciplinarian, a fan of boxing, and an alcoholic. Each quality impacted, in major ways, the man who would be the next to challenge Holmes.

Cooney had boxed since he was fifteen years old, and he moved out of the house when he was eighteen. A Golden Gloves champion, he was a hot amateur prospect because of his size and the obvious power in his left hook. As a pro he was trained by a Puerto Rican former fighter named Victor Valle, who, in some ways, became his father figure. His managers, on the other hand, clearly did not qualify for that positon.

Dennis Rappaport and Mike Jones were real estate brokers and poker buddies. Their boxing reputation was built on their ability to sign a few good fighters (the 1976 Olympic champion, Howard Davis, was one) and their headline-at-any-cost personalities. They demanded that one of their fighters, Ronnie Harris, who was a black Jew, be allowed to fight wearing a yarmulke. When the commission turned them down, they sued and got their headline.

"They were a pain in the ass," John Condon, president of Madison Square Garden Boxing, once told me. "I call them the Wacko Twins."

So did everyone else in boxing.

The Twins were born salesmen, and they soon figured out that they were selling knockout power. To sell it, your guy had to knock out other guys with big reputations. The easiest way to do that was to find, as opponents, guys whose legs had long since melted away at a pace that outstripped the notches on their guns.

The formula was to pay the once-upon-a-time fighters of stature enough to get them in for the beating. Cooney knocked out Jimmy Young in four rounds and Ron Lyle and Ken Norton each in one round—in succession, within a year. It did not matter to them that their fighter had learned almost nothing during the process. According to their agenda, this was enough to get a title fight. Winning it, to them, was of secondary importance.

The Holmes–Cooney fight should have been made a year or two later, but since the Wacko Twins fashioned it in conjunction with Don King, the pre-fight buildup conned America. They put together a kind of street corner three-card Monte game in which race, not talent, was the measuring stick. Rappaport marched forward, trumpeting, "There will be America, apple pie, Wheaties, and Gerry Cooney," and followed up with, "Not the white man but the right man." In Cooney, they created an opponent whom part of America rushed to embrace—one who was still lacking the boxing skills he needed for such a battle, one who was rushed in over his head into the fiery furnace as a pawn in a buildup that cast him in a role he didn't want.

In concert, the three key figures—King, Rappaport, and Jones—shamelessly stoked America's subliminal fires of racial fear, pseudo-racial pride, and a large dose of racial hatred. Together, they reached back more than seventy years to recreate what had always been an odious legacy in sports: the 1910 saga of the Great White Hope.

On July 4, 1910, a white former heavyweight champion named James J. Jeffries had come out of retirement to challenge Jack Johnson, the black title holder. The fight was not about Johnson's title; it was all about the color of his skin. When Johnson won, the victory triggered race riots in several cities.

It was now 1982. With the exception of the brief reign of Ingemar Johansson, there had not been a white heavyweight champion since Rocky Marciano retired in 1956. King immediately dubbed Cooney, "The Great White Hope."

From the moment of the buildup to June 11, 1982, the trio worked to sell tickets through red-hot animus for a fight in which each man would get a record ten million dollars. Their rhetoric sold tickets. It also drew both fighters into unwanted roles.

Holmes, bitter because memories of Muhammad Ali constantly overshadowed his achievements, joined in King's hot-air pronouncements. "[Cooney] is only here because he's white. I could fight four black fighters and make nothing, and one fight with him makes me millions. He never paid dues. Did he ever fight, like me, for sixty-three dollars?"

Cooney, meanwhile, was beginning to suspect a truth he had never considered before. "Dennis [Rappaport] and Mike [Jones] hated each other. Each of them talked about the other one to me. I felt like I had gone from my father, who had always been abusive to me, to even more turmoil. And I was pissed off about Holmes and King. I could never be [Holmes's] friend, and I hated the whole White Hope business."

But it wouldn't go away. "I remember there was a confrontation," Holmes told me. "I was finished working, and I was talking to you guys [the press] when they came in and demanded I leave the building, so I thought, *fuck them*. It pissed me off and I *went* and sat my ass right down there in the bleachers."

Looking back years later, Cooney told me, "I didn't trust them—Rappaport and Jones. I wanted to be the best fighter I could possibly be, but they gave me guys with great records who were over the hill. I was betrayed by that. I never got the chance to keep learning. They didn't care about me. They had another agenda. They just wanted the immediate big payday."

He had, indeed, come from a home with an abusive father. Tony Cooney was a construction worker who got up at 5:30 in the morning before work to supervise Cooney's road work. "I went from road work to school to the Long Island Railroad and onto a subway to the gym in Queens. That was my life every day. It wore me down. I was so tired that one day I was doing road work early in the morning, and the text thing I knew I was slumped on the curb sound asleep. My father caught me, and I got a beating for that.

"He never told me he loved me. One of the things he did tell me often was that I was nothing and that I would never amount to anything." As Cooney trained in the middle of turmoil, those words haunted him.

Rich Rose, a capable public relations guy, was brought in to help the Cooney camp. Rose explained, "We had just done a phone interview with *Sport Magazine* when Gerry turned to me and said, 'I want to make sure you understand something. You are only here because of Dennis and Mike. I don't like you, and I don't trust you—and I'll be watching you.'"

Neither camp had a monopoly on paranoia. What King, Rappaport, and Jones had created spread to other groups like the plague. "Dennis brought in twelve bodyguards—black belts, SWAT guys from LA, former fighters . . . whatever," Rose recalled. "No chambermaid was allowed to go into Gerry's room unless one of them accompanied her. Dennis even checked the vents in the air conditioners. One day, he went ballistic when a fruit basket was delivered to Cooney's, possibly because it did not come with a food taster."

Meanwhile, Holmes had brought in veteran trainers Ray Arcel and Eddie Futch. Arcel had a friendship with the chef at the Dunes Hotel next door to Caesars where the fighters lived. "From now on, no room service," Arcel told Holmes. "We go out the back way and through the Dunes kitchen to a room that will be set up for all your meals."

The media bought the whole deal, lock, stock, and racial animus. *Time Magazine* added to the fire. When it featured the upcoming fight, it put Cooney and Sylvester Stallone, whose *Rocky III* film had just been released, on the front cover. Larry Holmes, the world champion, was relegated to a picture inside.

The final press conferences were held separately. "It has come to such that we can't put them on the stage at the same time," explained King, who had contributed more than his share to the manufactured racial tensions.

Two nights before the fight, I had dinner with the Holmes camp in his room, where he calmly and logically produced the only conversation about race that had made sense all week.

"Look," he said, "You see what's happening. I can't speak to a single reporter without being asked about race. I am black and he is white, and all the talk in the world ain't gonna change that. But I get angry because the people who criticize this are the same people who keep bringing it up.

"Look around this room. Eddie Futch, my trainer, is black. Ray Arcel, my other trainer, is white. Louis Rodriquez, my friend over there, is Hispanic. My sister-in-law and my secretary at the end of the table are both white.

"All this talk is stupid. When I say Gerry Cooney is here because he's white, I am talking economics. That don't make me a racist. And what he says don't make him a racist either. You know what I really am?"

"No," I said.

"A hungry man, so let's eat."

Earlier in the day, the mood was different when I sat with Victor Valle. His job would be vastly different from that of Futch and Arcel, as Ray had explained: "We have a fighter who has been ready for a while now. All we have to do is keep him ready. Victor has a fighter who hasn't fought for some time and who really hasn't fought against quality. You could take a kangaroo or a bear and show him how to look like a boxer; people have done that. But until a man is there alone enough times, you just don't know. Nobody can be accomplished at anything without experience. We can plan with our fighter. I'm not sure what he can do with his."

When I interviewed Valle, those concerns were heightened by his own physical problems. There was a massive bruise on his left bicep where Cooney had accidentally slammed a right hand into him during a gym drill, rupturing the blood vessels. Earlier that day, during a drill on what to do if he were pinned on the ropes, Cooney accidently drove an elbow into Victor's stomach.

"I couldn't straighten up. I was paralyzed. I kept telling Gerry not to worry. It was only pain; maybe it makes a point about going on with pain. I hope so. But that's the easy part. You don't have time to worry during the day, but at night, when I am alone, yes, I worry. I won't lie to you. I see this fight over and over in my mind."

"Do you ever see your fighter making a bad mistake?" I asked.

"Of course. That's all I think about. I see things, and the next time I try to remind Gerry of what we must avoid. He and I are like family. I believe in him, but I don't sell Holmes short by any means."

Both Futch and Arcel had major concerns about what they saw in Holmes on the last day of sparring. The gym had been packed with Cooney supporters who hooted and jeered him. In a rage, he seemed to have left his marvelous jab back in the locker room. He beat his sparring partner, Jody Ballard, as though he were a Salvation Army bass drum, something he never did before.

The two trainers confronted him alone in the gym the next day. Futch said, "Larry, I don't know what happened in that sparring session, but Cooney is big and strong, and the jab can win it for you, so don't do something dumb. His left hook can put you down."

"So was Shavers," Holmes replied. "So was Norton. I'll keep the left in his face all night long."

The trainers exchanged glances. Arcel smiled. "He's ready."

When fight night came, it was almost a relief for everyone. The temperature had dropped from a blazing one hundred to eighty-nine degrees, and so had the rhetoric. Despite all the sound and fury, it was Holmes who said the one thing Cooney needed to hear to end all the madness. As they stood in the center of the ring, Mills Lane, the referee, said, "Touch 'em up, and let's get it won." Holmes looked Cooney squarely in the eyes and said, just loud enough to be heard by the other fighter above the roar of a Las Vegas record crowd of almost thirty thousand people, "Let's have a good fight."

"When he said that," Cooney told me, "it was the defining moment for me. The whole burden of all that bullshit was gone. We were just two fighters about to do what two fighters always do."

The fight separated the hard-working amateur from the polished professional.

In the first round, Holmes out-jabbed Cooney, jolting his head back, and ultimately landed a ferocious right to the head. At the bell, Valle told his fighter, "If that's all he has, he's shit, Gerry."

In the second round, they found out. After moving him around with the jab, Holmes confused Cooney and dropped him just as

Cooney prepared to throw the hook at Holmes's body. "I'm saying to myself," Cooney recalled, "what the hell am I doing here? Get up." He did so on unsteady legs, and the bell ended the round, a welcome relief. "He caught me because I would throw and not get out," Cooney said on hindsight. "I would stand in front of him with very little head movement."

Cooney fought well in the middle rounds, partially because he had settled down and partially because Holmes's new boxing shoes had begun to cause a huge blister on the soles of each foot, forcing him to pull back and totally rely on the jab. He was also starting to heed the advice of Futch, who thought he was getting careless.

"Box . . . keep on boxing," said Futch. "I don't want you to let him turn this into a brawl. He's young, and he's strong. Stick the jab and keep moving."

By round eight, Cooney was cut above the eye. It was clear to all but his loudest partisans and two of the three judges that he was losing the fight. Before the fight ended, Cooney would lose three points for low blows.

The absurd racial pressure that had earlier been placed on both men was enormous. What rational human being could possibly think a fighter could walk into a ring, with all the perils, pain, and emotion involved, and be fighting for anyone but himself and his family? The theory reached its nadir, which, in the framework of this fairy tale, was close to as low as you can get when Dennis Rappaport started to leave the ring just before the bell for the tenth round, a round during which Holmes would come off the ropes after playing possum and drive Cooney backwards with a series of combinations. As Cooney rose from his stool to face Holmes, his eye already cut, Rappaport shrieked at him, "America needs you . . . America needs you. Win for your dead father."

At the bell for round eleven, Valle implored, "Go out there and rough him up, Gerry, rough him up." But Cooney was done.

Rounds eleven and twelve turned into target practice for Holmes's hurting jab. One of Cooney's eyes was closing, and blood leaked from a cut above the other one.

The end came in the thirteenth. Holmes staggered him with a right, and Cooney summoned all he had left in the tank to throw the left hook by which his career had soared. There was nothing left behind it. Holmes's answer was staccato—left-right-right-right-left-right. Cooney reeled back. He clung to the ropes as Mills Lane moved in for a standing eight count. Valle sailed a towel into the ring and followed it by coming through the ropes, embracing Cooney, and shouting to the referee, "Enough . . . enough . . . no more."

That night, Larry Holmes and Gerry Cooney transcended a tawdry ocean of venom, spewed by the King-Rappaport-Jones axis that swept the country for some fifteen months prior, threatening to drown anything the nation had ever learned about race relations. The ones—both black and white—who were so determined to make this fight a proxy stand for race supremacy had not prevailed. The agony both fighters endured in the brutal heat for nearly thirty-nine emotional minutes was for their own prides and motivations, as opposed to the assigned roles in a tired and dangerous mythology that should have been sent to a dishonored grave centuries before. In the end, it was as each of them said in his own words when they bared their souls after.

"I didn't fight this fight for all the black people in America," Holmes said. "I fought it for myself and my family and the people who believed in me."

"I didn't care about the money," said Cooney, with sunglasses covering his battered eye, his voice beginning to break. "I fought it because I wanted to win . . . I wanted to win," he repeated slowly and then, in despair, banged the top of the table with his palm. "I fought my ass off."

Finally, here were the heroes who rescued the night. Gerry Cooney, who fought with an honor and courage that transcended his skills, but whose fate was pre-ordained. Mills Lane, the referee, who balanced the emotion and danger of what the judges could have turned into a time-bomb of a night with a superb officiating job. Victor Valle, whose love for the fighter he trained prompted him to rush into the ring to stop it—a lone sentinel of human emotion against the constant noise of the Wacko Twins. And Larry Holmes, who had weathered the ferocious power of Cooney's left hooks, that shook him; who had controlled the ring's geography; and who, in short, fought like the champion he was.

Cooney was not Rocky I, II, or even XII any more than Larry Holmes was earlier in his career. There is no such person, despite the hype surrounding this fight held under the backdrop of the world's largest American flag draped against the side of Caesars Palace and the million cheap words spoken to promote it. Cooney was Cooney, and when it was over, he had the kind of class that Rocky, the supposed patron saint of this fight, never had.

And Larry Holmes was Larry Holmes, who never hated Cooney in the first place. Free of the pressures from the fight buildup, he was wrong about only one thing. Cooney was as much a legitimate contender as a great many white and black Americans, as well as a collection of foreigners. Being Larry Holmes, he freely admitted this long after the fight. "In the years later," he said, "I argued with people who claimed Cooney was a bum. He wasn't. He was good enough to become a world champion if his people had only given him the chance to learn the way a fighter must. I'm surprised he never won a title."

The greatest irony of all amid all the racial fiction surfaced more than a decade after the fight. Because of the geographic gap between his family and distant relatives, Cooney would later take a DNA test to get a handle on his family history, which would reveal that his grandfather's mother was African American.

Enough, therefore, of the Wacko Twins' manufactured sound and fury of overt racism. Holmes and Cooney did what fighters do, leaving apologies unnecessary.

That's how we ought to remember it.

TEN

His Brother's Keeper: The Other Spinks

"I didn't have to be a professional boxer. There are other things I believe I could do."

—Michael Spinks

"I want to sit back and drink beer and watch these other heavyweights beat on each other. I neglected [my wife] Diane for ten years. Now I want to spend the next ten chasing her around our house."

—Larry Holmes, on his plans after Holmes–Spinks

The ugliness surrounding the promotion of his fight with Gerry Cooney was over. Now there was just one goal left to fulfill before he could retire. Larry Holmes was 40–0, and one of the most prized records in the history of boxing was within reach. Rocky Marciano had retired at 49–0, and no other heavyweight came close.

The path to equaling that mark was clearly there. It required Holmes's spectacular jab, the gold standard for the punch, combined with what in boxing is politely known as "creative matchmaking." The latter was much in evidence in seven of his next eight fights. He became the first heavyweight champion of the International Boxing Federation (IBF), abdicated the World Boxing Council (WBC) title, and avoided unfavorable mandated bouts. Of those eight fights, only one was with a legitimate contender, Tim Witherspoon, a future champion, who forced him to use everything he had to earn a controversial split decision. Now, Holmes was 48–0. For the historic potential forty-ninth win, he reached out for a manufactured contender with some credentials.

He found him in Leon Spinks's twenty-nine-year-old brother, Michael. If Holmes wanted the benefit of shrewd matchmaking in this the record-tying match, it seemed he had come to the right place. Michael Spinks was the champion of the light heavyweight division, where the maximum weight is 175 pounds. In contrast, there are no weight restrictions on the heavyweight division. Holmes was a taller and much heavier man. Even if Spinks could bulk up, he would still be conceding a weight advantage to the champion of at least twenty pounds or more. No light heavyweight champion before him had won the heavyweight title since Bob Fitzsimmons knocked out James J. Corbett in 1897 in Carson City, Nevada.

There were times when it appeared that challenging the heavyweight title was the absolute last thing on Michael Spinks's mind. Unlike his brother, Leon, Michael planned to quit boxing after they both won their Olympic gold medals (in the light heavyweight division for Leon and middleweight for Michael) in Montreal in 1976. Michael did not like to fight. The Spinks brothers grew up in St. Louis in the Pruitt-Igoe Housing Project—a public housing division so lawless and dangerous that ultimately the City Housing Authority declared it unsafe for its residents, ultimately evacuating and razing the complex. For the kids, Pruitt-Igoe was a daily, violent struggle for survival, and Michael told those who asked that he would not turn professional after the Olympics. However, his bond with Leon was too strong to ignore, and at Leon's nagging, he agreed to return to the sport.

I first got to know Michael in early 1978 because I was looking for Leon, who had just beaten Ali and embarked on an alcohol-fueled odyssey. Their mother, Kate, said Leon and Michael planned to visit her new apartment at the Durst-Webbe Housing Project, and told me to come around midnight.

The first cab driver refused to take me there. The second agreed, but only with the understanding that he wouldn't wait for me. Once inside the compound, I kept pressing the elevator button until a little girl said, "It's broken, mister, it's always broken. If you want to go to the third floor the stairs are over there."

As I climbed the stairs, the first thing I noticed was that all of the lights were out. It occurred to me that this would not be a very cool place to die. I have never moved that quickly any time in my life before nor since.

When I arrived, Sister Kay (as Kate was called) pulled me inside before anyone could see me. The one-bedroom apartment was packed with people. To this day, I have no idea where they had come from. Sister Kay told me that Leon had not called and probably wouldn't show but that Michael was on his way with a childhood friend from the projects named Nick Miranda, who wanted to manage him. They were coming to get Sister Kay's approval.

When they arrived, we were introduced. Then, Sister Kay raced through an opening-pitch soliloquy. "We got to pray on this," she said, placing the contract on the floor and dropping to her knees. There followed a large crash, which is the sound twenty or so sets of knees make in unison when they hit the floor to pray.

It went on for a long time. Each time I thought she was going to end there came another burst—"and besides that, Father, we need to know . . . ." I have had bone disease in my right knee from birth, and I was about to say, *Sorry, that's all folks.* When she came to the part of her prayer that pleaded, "Can I get an amen to this," my amen would have done honor to any amen corner in any church on the planet.

As I struggled to my feet, Michael said, "I'll give you a ride back to the hotel." I was so relieved I almost offered another amen.

Looking back, it was a great thing that Leon never showed. Back at the Chase-Park Plaza, which had an all-night coffee shop, Michael, Miranda, and I had a productive conversation. "I never wanted to turn pro," Michael told me. "I mean, the excitement at the Olympics and the feeling of accomplishment was special. But professional boxing—I'm not even sure I want it now. There are other things I believe I could do. But Leon, well, when Leon decided to make the move, we talked it over. I'm not the smartest guy in the world, but I can read and I can write and I can add. Leon is, well, I didn't want to leave him out there alone."

What happened was that as Leon fought more, Michael fought less, always looking over Leon's shoulder to see if anyone was trying to harm him. And a lot of people tried.

The statement was prophetic. Michael tried to be with his brother as much as possible so that there would be at least one set of eyes in Leon's camp that had his back. It explained why, in 1978 and again in 1979, Michael fought a total of three times. Leon continued to drink and train as though it was a weekend job, and eventually it all fell apart. There was nothing else Michael could do for his brother but try to put together the pieces of his own life.

Michael Spinks made money. He spoke well. He became the light heavyweight champion. When he came to Las Vegas for the fight against Larry Holmes on September 21, 1985, on the biggest stage boxing can have, he played no games with the media; he told the truth.

"How can you handle a jab like Holmes has?" I asked him.

"I don't know. I've never been hit by it. It hurts, I guess. I'll stop and think—so that's what it is. But let's wait and see on that; I am sure you will know the same time I do."

That afternoon, I checked the sports books at a couple of hotels and the lowest odds against Spinks were 5–1. When I informed Holmes of it, he said, "Actually, it shouldn't be on the board at all. I've thought about it a million times, and I still don't see a way he can beat me. On the other hand, I sure as hell am not going to give him one. The only way he can get into this fight is if I let him in—and I won't.

"If he comes in heavy, he's a fool because a man has to fight at his natural weight. If he comes in light, I will beat him down early. I hit like a heavyweight, and if he hits me he's still a lighter guy hitting a bigger one.

"But I'm not putting him down here. Why have I been in this position so long? It's because I don't do drugs, I don't run the streets, and I know how much my family means to me. But understand, I am not putting him down when I say this: He's a champion. I never felt it was right for one champion to discredit another one. On Saturday, we'll try to take each other's heads off. That's business. I would like to feel I could be his friend later on."

This was a title fight with no town criers to fuel it with the phony anger of Holmes–Cooney, no Ali to turn it into comedic theater, and no exotic setting like Central Africa or Malaysia. Instead, the ancillary cheerleading came from a totally unexpected source.

The Marciano Family was in deep prayer, and they offered loud rhetoric with reasons Rocky's record should not be broken. It paid no heed to the logical, historical truth that records are, indeed, made to be broken. It ignored the fact that records are the measuring sticks by which we determine our heroes' places in America's pantheon of icons. The Marciano family was so intent on making it a holy war that it didn't understand that even if Holmes tied the record, America would continue to honor Marciano for setting it.

Holmes wasn't fighting Marciano, but the Marcianos were fighting Holmes. They showed up in Vegas allegedly to promote a movie about the late champion's life, setting their own record for tasteless behavior at a boxing match (if such a thing is even possible) by announcing they were lighting religious candles to aid their prayers for a Holmes defeat. Holmes conversely matched the sentiment during the post-fight press conference, when he said of Rocky Marciano, "I'm thirty-five, fighting much younger guys. He was twenty-five fighting much older guys. Rocky Marciano couldn't carry my jock strap." After a brief exchange, he apologized to the Marciano family, though anyone with a sense of propriety would have realized that none of them had any business in the room in the first place.

Despite this, the week before the fight was, for the most part, without rumors or incidents right up until the weigh-in. It was a meaningless ceremony since the fighters did not have to make the target weight. Godzilla and Tom Thumb could have stepped on the scale and each would have qualified to fight for the heavyweight title.

Michael Spinks weighed in at an even two hundred pounds, more than twenty pounds above his previous top fighting weight. Then it was Larry Holmes's turn, and what seemed like 2,003 Nevada Commission and International Boxing Federation hangers-on rushed to get their face time as the TV cameras recorded. Someone proudly boomed into the microphone, "Larry Holmes, 121.50 pounds," prompting a bystander to comment: "Either someone doesn't know how to count or else Larry trained as though he were auditioning for the lead role in Gandhi."

After serious consultation, the officials decided the actual weight was 221.50, an indication that Holmes had not seen a single dessert he didn't like that month.

This is what we knew during the countdown to fight time: We knew that the logical assumption for Spinks was to match Holmes jab for jab, keep what fighters call his range (enough distance to allow for punching leverage), get inside, do damage, and then get the hell out as fast as he could. He would have to overcome his tendency to lose balance when he backed up, the residue of an old leg injury.

He would also have to find a way to deal with the fact that in a genuine heavyweight against light heavyweight match-up, time and time again, the bigger guy had a massive edge. I saw it when Bob Foster, the best one-punch fighter among modern light heavyweights, cut and staggered Ali but was stopped in the next round. It was the same story when he fought Frazier. Foster hit Frazier so hard that he stopped him in his tracks, during a time when nobody could make him do that. In the next round, Frazier hit him with a ferocious hook and Foster went down so hard he broke his ankle.

On paper, therefore, the odds against Spinks seemed correct. It would be up to Holmes to give it away by failing to press his weight advantage, or if he fell into an old habit of coasting at the wrong time, or if time and the calendar itself had already taken too much out of him—something most of us didn't think about.

The work was done. Nobody would get any smarter or any stronger when the bell finally rang. It was as Spinks said the last time we talked: "I've said as much as I can say, and I've heard as much as I can hear. I cannot think of a question I haven't been asked. There really is nothing left to do except go out and do it."

So they did.

In the first three rounds, it appeared as though the underdog's grasp was a lot shorter than the underdog's reach. Holmes came out and fired jab after jab. Spinks had no answer. When they clinched, Holmes wrestled him away as though it were a father-son tug-o-war at the Elks picnic. There seemed to be nothing to indicate that this would not be a textbook fight with an early ending in store.

But in the fourth round, when Holmes came out with the jab for the knockout that would ensure his tying Marciano's record, a strange thing happened. To me, it appeared as though the calendar had finally reached out and encased his body clock in a grip he could not break.

He was wild. He was awkward. And never again in the fight would he regain the fluid rhythm and pace he had set over the first three rounds. In short, he had accomplished what he had been so sure he would not do: he invited Michael Spinks back into the fight.

The middle rounds were awful. It was as though one couldn't fight and the other wouldn't fight. In the thirteenth and four-teenth rounds, Holmes maneuvered Spinks into the corner where he wanted him, as he had done earlier in the evening. However, each time Holmes tried to unleash the right hand that was made for such situations, the calendar intervened and locked the glove into a parade rest as though it were filled with 140 pounds of sand. There was also something else none of us knew: Holmes was fighting with a pinched nerve that triggered serious pain whenever he threw the right hand.

And there was nothing the champion could do about it. Sooner or later, the calendar makes old men of all of us. It was not so much that this was Spinks's time, but rather more that Holmes's had passed.

It was the most peculiar of evenings. That's not surprising when you consider that the match was made by Don King and Butch Lewis, a pair of rival promoters and crazy personalities who often waged war against each other, seemingly from their psychiatrists' couches. Would a promoter come to the fight wearing a white din-ner jacket, a red bow tie, and no shirt? Where else would a fighter actually stop fighting and scream at a promoter, as Spinks did to Lewis, who was shrieking hysterical, incoherent instructions to him? ("I can't," Spinks yelled back. "He's holding and I'm running away.")

And where else would the other fighter stand still and watch?

It would have been nice if we could recall the structure of this particular fight and rhapsodize about the cutting jabs and thunder-ous left hooks—but there weren't any. Spinks fought exactly as his brother, Leon, did when he won the title from Ali. He threw strange punches from strange angles, none of which hurt but most of which found their way to the judges' scorecards.

They rendered a unanimous decision for Spinks (I had a draw). Both the Associated Press and United Press International scored it for Holmes.

Holmes, though bitterly disappointed, was realistic. He knew in his heart that he had not been at his best. He also knew that the list of active and impressive light heavyweight fighters in the country is shorter than that of surviving World War I vets. Spinks had cashed the longest of long shot lottery tickets.

Afterward, we asked him if he was thinking about a title defense.

"I don't know," he said. "To tell you the truth, I never expected to win it."

Spinks's first title defense was pre-ordained. Holmes, who had wanted to retire, now couldn't. These two had unfinished business, especially based on the closeness of the score cards and the rounds that could have gone either way. The rematch was set seven months later for April 19, 1986.

Right up until that first shocking night in this same town, Spinks had been the light heavyweight champion, locked into a division where the money was minimal, and the recognition zero. The best-in-show at the Westminster Kennel Club competition got more attention. In truth, if Spinks had any claim to recognition before he beat Larry Holmes, it was simply for being "the other Spinks." But strange things happen in this business. If they didn't, then Spinks would not be making his first defense against a guy much larger and stronger than himself who had never lost until their first fight.

The week before the rematch, a brand new Michael Spinks arrived in Las Vegas. Gone was the soft-spoken challenger with self-doubts. In his place stood the newly-minted IBF heavyweight champion, unveiling a brand new set of biceps in a larger frame. Spinks had come to town. As James Brown used to sing, *Papa's got a brand new bag.*

Of course, as IBF champion Spinks knew he owned only a well-splintered chard of the heavyweight title. He had come to Vegas with the knowledge that he had no share in the WBA or WBC title. However, he also knew that HBO had announced it would finance a super tournament among the best heavyweights to select the champion of them all, a kind of soap opera that could well have been entitled "Cable TV Saves the Whales."

Spinks was not supposed to beat Holmes the first time, but he had done the impossible. If he beat him again, it would earn him a ticket to ride on the gravy train from which HBO would anoint the new Big Kahuna. It was incentive enough.

"The impact of that fight is now on him, not me," Spinks said in his first informal press conference. "He has become Humpty Dumpty. All of a sudden, somebody threw a big boulder at his glass house and it came crashing down. Like I said, Humpty Dumpty. After that crash, nobody can put him together again."

Spinks was right. The pressure was on Holmes for reasons far beyond the fact that he had lost a decision to an overstuffed light heavyweight. He had come to the town where winners ultimately lose and losers never quit. Neither was he the first to do so, nor would he be the last. It didn't matter whether he could throw a fastball a hundred miles an hour, hit the three-pointer from the other end of the court, or earn the heavyweight championship. All of the men who came to fight eventually lost what had earlier made them American legends. It is the same as the singer who loses his voice, gets laughed off the stage, points to the orchestra, and shouts, "Shoot them all—and start with the piano player." In my mind, Holmes–Spinks II had become a fight that Spinks could win on tactics and conditioning—or lose if Holmes's memory carried him through one last heroic effort, and if he succeeded in making his jab golden one last time.

With all the talk and the new HBO incentive, we did not actually get a true, new fight that night. It turned out to be a piece of carbon paper that proved nothing. The questions it posed were all left unanswered. Had Michael Spinks beat a legend twice, or had he been given two tainted gifts? Had Larry Holmes been victimized twice, or, as often happens, were both fights close enough that he was kicked in the ass by Father Time, when all he needed was one last blast from the past?

You could have scored this one with twenty different arithmetical combinations and nobody could say with certainty that you were wrong. You could have given it to either fighter, or called it a draw, or thrown your scorecard up in the air and demanded that everyone start over again. Anyone who knows anything about the strange business that is boxing would tell you the exact same thing. It wasn't a prize fight at all. Metaphorically, it was a Chinese restaurant menu with columns A and B—and with either fighter you got sweet and sour sauce at no extra cost. Certainly, throughout the evening each fighter had his highs and lows, but neither overwhelmed the other.

So, what did I see at the Las Vegas Hilton Center that night? What I know is that Spinks won a highly controversial split decision. And when you win, you keep the title.

Holmes, as expected, came tearing across the ring. He pinned Spinks against the ropes and, during a subsequent clinch, hurled him to the canvas like a sack of potatoes. He dominated the early rounds on a blend of brute force and a barrage of sweet jabs, piling up points at a price that the calendar and its passing years would subsequently extract from him. Spinks was hit with a furious right hand to the head, but he heard no alarm bells. Surely he must have thought, "Well, the hell with him. He just proved he can't hurt me."

In rounds five and six, Spinks came forward behind his own jab, which may not have hurt Holmes, but it was definitely a distraction worth the points. The early sting of Holmes's punches was gone. Now, if Spinks hung in there, all pain was negotiable.

Spinks backed Holmes up with two hooks and a right cross in the sixth, and landed six straight jabs in the eighth. In a competitive sense, there was little to choose from between the two. In the fourteenth, Spinks snapped Holmes's head back with the second of two right hands, but a tremendous counter right by Holmes was far more damaging, hurting Spinks and sending him reeling across the ring.

Before the last round, Holmes sat in his corner with an ice pack over one eye as Richie Giachetti, his trainer, desperately tried to massage at least one of the lost years back into his body for a last effort.

In the fifteenth, Holmes landed the same right hand in the same part of Spinks's head, coming within a whisper of ending the bout. At the bell, I didn't know who I thought had won until I rechecked my scorecard. I had Holmes ahead by a point. The judges split in favor of Spinks. He kept the title.

I came away with several conclusions: First, it was close enough that either man could have won it.

Second, Holmes would have easily knocked Spinks out two years earlier.

Despite what his dietitian and the Hilton Center weighing scale said, Michael Spinks was still a light heavyweight with a light heavyweight's punch.

Michael Tyson would prove the point during a brief appearance against Spinks. Tyson's power and Spinks lack thereof ended the charade in just 91 seconds.

ELEVEN

An HBO Dream and the Road that Led to Mike Tyson

"I grew up around the corner from Ebbets Field. Baseball was a part of my life as a Brooklyn kid. If they could hold a World Series, then why couldn't we hold the World Series of Boxing?"

—Seth Abraham

And the heavyweight champion of the world is . . . is . . . well, who the hell knows? From the moment Leon Spinks upset Muhammad Ali in February 1978, an incredible roster of fifteen contenders and pretenders staked claims to the heavyweight championship of the planet. A tsunami of alphabet soup sanctioning organizations, each using an assortment of acronyms, made enormous money grabs that would change boxing forever. Their names were ludicrous: World Boxing Council, World Boxing Association, International Boxing Federation—none of which was global, and none of which was respected as a council, an association, or a Federation. More than one of their ersatz titles often carried the suspicion that they had arrived cash-on-delivery because of the private fiefdoms and sanctioning fees these bodies fiercely guarded and collected from each title fight—or, as they might put it at The Wharton School, *the more titles, the more money.*

Uniting them under one tent was a problem fit for King Solomon. But since the "baby" had already been sliced three ways, a far greater power was required, one that would eventually be capable of wielding an influence in every home in America.

Seth Abraham was the standard bearer of Home Box Office's sports division. This was at a time when an American Broadcasting Company championship boxing tournament, fueled by phony *Ring Magazine* records and ratings, had been revealed as corrupt; a time when television sponsors sought to remove themselves from any association with boxing; a time when HBO was moving toward the eventual money tree of in-home pay-per-view.

Most of all, HBO was paying what was then considered well above market value to sign the fighters needed. Now, Abraham would turn a private pipe dream into a reality and bring his company an even bigger advantage. He had a plan that required more money, nerve, and genuine diplomacy. "I was born around the corner from Ebbets Field," he explained. "The year of my birth, the Dodgers were in a subway World Series with the Yankees. I played college baseball. The World Series was a big deal for me. When the heavyweight championship split three ways, I thought, *This is our chance to get it all.* A World Series–type of boxing tournament: seven World Series fights (sort of like baseball). Hopefully, we'd find a way to get the three governing bodies to agree."

It was an idea that began to move toward fruition on a night in 1985 when Don King visited Abraham to peddle a heavyweight fight between his WBC champion, Pinklon Thomas, and Mike Weaver. They met in Chinatown at the Canton Restaurant. King was intrigued, but he still pushed for his original WBC proposal. "I didn't reject it as a fight," Abraham recalled. "Thomas was a good fighter, but I couldn't see what it meant to the heavyweight division. I asked [King] about my World Series plan and said we couldn't do it unless we had all the champions. He asked me what this would be worth in dollars. I told him I didn't know because we still didn't know the fighters. But I said that whatever it is really worth, HBO will pay.

"When we met again, it was at my home in Greenwich Village in October. Don flew in from Cleveland and my wife made a lobster dinner. We watched the Cardinals and Royals in the World Series and then talked some more about my 'World Series.'"

At the time, King and Butch Lewis, who managed the IBF champion Michael Spinks, were in a violent feud. Abraham reminded King that his idea wouldn't work without all three champions. King gave it some thought and agreed it might be worth a try. They stayed up until 2 a.m. drawing, discarding, and redrawing brackets.

"I still had to deal with the heads of the three governing bodies," Abraham said. "Before we quit figuring, I wanted to get something else clear. I had been watching Tyson in places like Albany and Utica. He was just beginning and couldn't be in the tournament because he was ranked as low as the twenty-second or twenty-third, but I wanted him on the undercards. We signed for three bouts, and it helped King make up his mind. He didn't have Tyson, who was managed by Jimmy Jacobs and Bill Cayton, but realized that Tyson would bring in more pay-per-view money." And, since HBO would pay Tyson, Don would be getting three free fights and better cards.

With King already on board, Butch Lewis joined in negotiations in the big dining hall and conference room at HBO. "I felt like Henry Kissinger," Abraham recalled. "But it wasn't Israel and Palestine. It was King and Butch on opposite sides of the room."

On Christmas morning at 10:30 a.m., Lewis, Lewis's father, King, Abraham, three other HBO officials, and an army of lawyers sat down to finalize the deal. It took them three meals and nine and a half hours before the tournament finally jumped off the drawing board. The event drew tremendous heat from the media. HBO, they said, was trying to monopolize the whole business. Others questioned the credentials of some of the fighters, most notably the Norwegian Steffen Tangstad. But the show went on.

In 1986, Tim Witherspoon beat Tony Tubbs for the WBA title. Witherspoon stopped England's Frank Bruno, and then lost to a total outsider named James "Bonecrusher" Smith. Trevor Berbick upset Pinklon Thomas for the WBC Crown. Spinks, who had won his rematch with Holmes, easily defeated Tangstad to defend his IBF title.

Then, Abraham's plan was in danger of falling apart. Butch Lewis pulled Spinks out of the tournament and had him resign the IBF title. Lewis's plan was to wait until the tournament was over so he could extract more money from future fights. Consequently, HBO sued Spinks for breach of contract, but Spinks won because a judge ruled that his lack of the IBF title made his contract with HBO null and void. Determined to have an eventual unification bout, Abraham and King accepted an IBF box-off between Tony Tucker and Buster Douglas, which Tucker won.

And what of young Mike Tyson, the magical mystery contender who had been consigned to an undercard status? Almost without fanfare, but totally on knockout power, he had moved from number 22 to a spot in the top 10. It was now the final stages of entering the HBO tournament. Spinks had just pulled out, and Buster Douglas had been substituted for him. When Trevor Berbick beat Douglas, Tyson was named as the last entry.

Tyson's storyline was far too powerful to ignore. He was the last fighter who would ever be trained by Cus D'Amato, a boxing mentor who spoke in parables and wrapped himself in an impenetrable cloak of paranoia.

Hidden away in Catskill, New York, in a house populated by aspiring fighters, D'Amato had always been a man who dealt in mysteries. I first met him when he trained heavyweight champion Floyd Patterson and middleweight contender José Torres. During those early days, he spoke constantly about the mob and how no fighter of his would ever fight one of their puppets. Of course, the question soon became "which mob," when we learned of his own association with friends of "Fat Tony" Salerno.

Still, D'Amato persisted in his party line, and Torres suffered for it. During their association, Torres rarely fought and never tried for the middleweight title. While D'Amato knew more about the fighters in the circuit than most other trainers—their strengths, weaknesses, and, most of all, fears—he was also totally paranoiac. Once, when I interviewed Torres at Madame Bey's Training Camp in the countryside of Summit, New Jersey, D'Amato berated me two weeks later: "What are you doing hanging around my fighter? You don't call him or see him unless you call me first." After Patterson lost to Liston, Torres left D'Amato and went on to become the light heavyweight champion of the world.

Since those days, D'Amato had retired to Catskill, New York, where he and his companion, Camille Ewald, lived in a house that was a kind of training camp for aspiring young, amateur fighters. One of them was Teddy Atlas, who became a trainer under his tutelage. Together, they ran the Catskill Boxing Club.

Occasionally, Bill Cayton and Jimmy Jacobs, managers who knew D'Amato, would send fighters like Wilfredo Benítez, Edwin Rosario, and Cyclone Hart to train there. But for the most part, D'Amato was resigned to the fact that his glory days were over. He was Don Quixote without a cause. He spent more time watching television shows like *Barney Miller* and less time in the Catskill Boxing Club gym, where he left the teaching to Atlas, whom he called the "Young Master." He became the old man of the mountain, living on memories, aware that the dance was over.

At this point in D'Amato's life, withdrawn from the world in which he used to live, he would drop by the gym once week. Atlas had learned well, but he knew he needed more. Though he pleaded with D'Amato to spend more time at the gym with him and the aspiring kids, something had left the old campaigner. D'Amato still believed in his passion to marry the physical and mental attributes of young fighters to create winners, but had lost through attrition what had once kindled the fire within.

Then, he received a phone call.

Bobby Stewart, a light heavyweight Golden Gloves champion, had known D'Amato during his amateur days. A competent but unspectacular pro before he retired, he now worked as a youth counselor at the Tryon Residential Center for Boys.

One of the inmates was a boy named Mike Tyson. Tyson had been arrested thirty times before he got to Tryon. He was only twelve years old at the time, but weighed 190 pounds and was a self-proclaimed badass. His street history seemed to support his contention. As part of his duties, Stewart supervised inmates in the ring during their recreation time.

In Tyson, Stewart saw size, aggression, and the bottom line requirements to be a boxer. In Stewart, Tyson saw a man with the knowledge of a way of life that intrigued him. He wanted desperately to learn to box, rather than just fight.

A strange, unspoken pact was formed between the two. In order to learn what Stewart had to give, Tyson played the part of a model inmate and lived within the institutional rules. In return, Stewart taught him what he knew—as long as Tyson behaved. When the ex-fighter had taught him all he had to offer, he called D'Amato and asked if both of them could come to Catskill to get Atlas's opinion.

"On the appointed day, Stewart and Tyson arrived in a Tryon van," Atlas recalled. "Because we didn't have anyone big enough to box with Tyson, Stewart would do the sparring." According to Atlas, his first impression was that he was looking at a child in a man's body. Tyson wasn't sure what was expected of him, but he knew instinctively that this was some kind of audition he wanted desperately to pass.

Through sheer will, Tyson forced Stewart to spar harder than he wanted. "So here was this kid in the ring with a twenty-seven-year-old man, and he did enough to push the retired boxer past where he wanted to go." Almost out of self-defense, Stewart gave Tyson a bloody nose.

"Tyson wanted another round," Atlas recalled, "but D'Amato and I had seen enough. I told him it was enough. He was very strong-willed. D'Amato was watching us, and I knew I had to establish a line of command if I was going to train him, so I told him absolutely no, and when he argued back I yelled at him to get out of the ring *now*. He did.

"Looking back, it occurs to me that he was rehearsing for something that would change his life. We knew he had innate ability and intelligence. What we needed to find out was whether he was tough and determined, and he proved he was in that session."

After the workout, Atlas told D'Amato that he saw the spark in the kid. D'Amato agreed. "Young Master," he said, "you saw it all. This kid could be your first heavyweight champion."

Atlas hadn't realized it at the time, but in his heart, D'Amato had already begun to substitute the word *my* for *your*. D'Amato began to scheme toward getting Tyson into his house and under his control. It began with weekend visits approved by Tryon and a social worker named Mrs. Coleman.

"During one weekend visit," Atlas recalled, "Mike, who knew what Cus had in mind and who badly wanted it, actually outperformed reality. It was Sunday dinner and the table, as usual, was loaded with food. Camille asked Mike to pass the potatoes.

"In his haste, Mike jumped up to bring them to her. When he jumped, his knees hit the underside of the table. It tilted, and the food began to slip over the side. Camille yelled for somebody to grab the meat, and the whole group was scrambling to keep all that food from falling. Tyson said over and over, 'Oh my God, I'm sorry.' But I was looking at Cus, and all Cus kept saying was, 'Look at those legs. Look at them. My God. What power in them.'

"Eventually, Cus got him as a ward of the state and put him in school, where he was nothing but trouble. He'd throw a book at a teacher or get a girl in a corner and touch her, and every time he was about to be expelled (which he ultimately was), Cus would go over to the school and square things."

As a fighter, Tyson continued to learn and grow. Jimmy Jacobs sent him films of great fighters, which he studied. He watched them hour after hour. He had an innate intellectual quest for that kind of knowledge.

While Atlas continued to train Tyson in the physical side of boxing, D'Amato remained his emotional mentor, lecturing him on what he could be if only he avoided distractions. "If you are going into the ring with a two-hundred-pound guy in front of you," he instructed Tyson, as he had with countless fighters before him, "you better be thinking of nothing else—in and out of the ring." Neither D'Amato nor anyone else involved in the care and training of Mike Tyson realized how prophetic the statement would ultimately become.

D'Amato taught, shaped, and sometimes overprotected Tyson. He lectured him on the need to focus, how to turn his fears into those of the opponent's, and what the stakes in life were if he progressed. He also explained that Sonny Liston had won a lot of fights by intimidating his opponents before they got into the ring.

Tyson won the regional, and then the national, Junior Olympics. On a bus ride during one of the trips, Atlas overheard a young amateur heavyweight tell another, "You think you beat me. Well,

you didn't. I let you win. I let you because," and here he pointed at
Tyson, "I didn't want to fight that animal."

"Tyson heard it, too," said Atlas, "and he said to me, 'We got 'em,
Teddy. We got 'em.'"

The master plan remained on target—or so they thought.

Then, all hell broke loose when Tyson broke one of Atlas's prime
gym rules. There were as many as twenty or thirty kids working in
the Catskill Boxing Club. Atlas was relentless in his belief that there
was more than boxing at stake for some of them. His edict was,
"Show me every report card. If you fail a subject, you are out of this
gym until you bring that grade up. There are no exceptions."

There was a lot of loyalty between the kids and their young
trainer. Because of that, some of them would tell Atlas things like,
"Mike got in trouble at school today." One day, they informed him
that Tyson had been expelled. It was news to Atlas. D'Amato, who
had known this, had kept it from him. D'Amato was torn between
loyalty to the trainer he had mentored and the fighter whom he
knew was his ticket back to one last hurrah, a fighter who would also
be heavyweight boxing's future. All of a sudden, according to Atlas,
D'Amato and Kevin Rooney (who would later succeed Atlas) were
secretly going to the gym in the morning hours before he arrived.

The explosion between them was inevitable. Atlas confronted
D'Amato and demanded to know why he hadn't told him of Tyson's
expulsion, The decibel level elevated. "Never mind. Never mind,"
D'Amato shouted. "You don't need to know anything about it."

"Now you say I don't need to know," Atlas yelled back. "You
have me train this kid. You tell me he's my responsibility, and now
you say I don't need to know. All of a sudden, he does something
wrong, and it's not my responsibility. Where is the consistency?"

Inch by inch, Atlas's tenure was coming to an end. At the finish,
it wouldn't end with a whimper, and it wouldn't end with a bang. It
would be in the echo of a sudden pistol shot.

D'Amato was now, more than ever, both mentor and, in Atlas's view, enabler. Atlas described the end this way: "I was on the way out, even though I was the one who had disciplined [Tyson] and tried to get him to behave in school. Now, he was a street kid again and I realized I had no power over him anymore. As a street kid, it gave him pleasure to hurt people. I believe that was because he could now go to Cus and win. I believe that's why he decided to hurt my family.

"I was living in an apartment by then with my wife and her kid sister. I came home one night and heard my wife's eleven-year-old sister crying in the bedroom. My wife is saying, 'Don't tell Teddy,' and now I'm shouting, 'Don't tell Teddy what?'

"[Tyson] had tried to force himself on my sister-in-law. I'm out the door. My friend had a club, and I knew he slept upstairs with a gun under his mattress. I grabbed it, and now I'm going to look for Tyson. I find him getting out of a cab in front of the gym. I grab him and put him up against the building. I tell him, "You wanna abuse people? It's not okay, and you have to know that if you ever come near my family again.' And I put the gun in his ear and cock it. I say, 'You have to understand you won't talk to me or see me the next time. You won't hear me, and you won't see me, because you won't ever hear or see anything again.'

"Then I took the gun out of his ear, put it next to his head, and shot it in the air. A week or two later, I took my family and left."

It wasn't until three decades later that Tyson realized the rage he had directed toward Atlas had run its course. By then, Atlas was a boxing analyst for ESPN, working a fight card on which Tyson was the promoter in name. During a break between bouts at the Turning Stone Resort Casino, Atlas heard a voice coming from behind him, saying, "Teddy, are you still mad at me? I was wrong. I was wrong. I'm sorry." Then Tyson stuck his hand out and said, "Please, please, shake my hand."

Atlas said nothing. The two stared at each other, and then Atlas took it.

Knowing the roller coaster ride that has always been Tyson's ups, downs, and explosions, I asked Atlas if he actually believed him.

Atlas thought about it. "I believe he meant it in the moment," he said.

Looking back at Mike Tyson's professional life, that scene was only a minor subtext that changed little. Because he wanted one more champion so badly, D'Amato pretty much let Tyson do as he pleased.

From the moment Bobby Stewart brought Tyson to Catskill, there were other players in the game who were in fact about to turn the greening of Mike Tyson into a well-financed business plan. Jimmy Jacobs, D'Amato's former roommate, was a collector of fight films and a director. His boss and partner was Bill Cayton, whose massive library of professional boxing films was almost a virtual monopoly. Cayton, who was intrigued by Tyson, agreed to finance his living expenses with D'Amato. Jacobs and Cayton agreed to be co-managers.

Atlas's departure changed the rules of the game. Now D'Amato was back in action, reaching for one last moment at the top of the mountain. Left without Atlas's dominant discipline rules, Tyson was free to do whatever he wanted outside the ring. In concert, D'Amato with his brain, Jacobs with his connections, Cayton with his money, and Tyson with his fists were bound for glory.

Kevin Rooney was now the trainer, again under the tutelage of D'Amato. In 1984, Tyson failed to make the Olympic team. D'Amato knew that Father Time had suddenly run a stopwatch on him and decided to stop playing around for medals.

For months, D'Amato had struggled with a nagging, often uncontrollable, chest cough. He sloughed it off to others in the house as inconsequential, but he probably knew it was more serious than he indicated. Now it was as though, through some foreboding, he had placed himself and his protégé on an urgent schedule. It was time to launch Tyson's career.

TWELVE

The Day the Heavyweight Champion Cried

"I want this fight. I want to fight Michael
Spinks. It's unfinished business. So make it."

—*Mike Tyson*

On March 6, 1984, Tyson made his debut at the Empire State Convention Center in Albany. The opponent was a novice heavyweight by the name of Hector Mercedes who had fought three professional bouts and lost them all. At the opening bell, Tyson seemed to explode out of his corner. Mercedes lasted less than a round.

Tyson went on a virtually unopposed spree, winning twenty-two of twenty-four bouts by knockout, with only two opponents going the distance. By then, Seth Abraham and HBO had Tyson on their world tournament undercard. Mike Tyson was the heavyweight the world awaited, propelled by one simple fact: He was the prototype heavyweights used to be all about. He knocked people out, bringing to the minds of fight fans a Louis, a Marciano, or a Liston. That thought process was not lost on Abraham. Dramatic knockouts mean viewers, viewers mean ratings, and, in the far more lucrative world of pay-per-view, Tyson's role as a warrior would mean one hell of a lot of money.

"In the collective mind of our potential audience," Abraham said, "the undisputed heavyweight champion of the world is the baddest man on the planet."

What that meant was, with his sheer knockout power, Tyson would be the punctuation mark at the finish that would justify HBO's heavyweight tournament. On September 6, 1985, Tyson fought his last fight on the HBO undercard, knocking out Akonzo Alfonzo Ratliff.

In less than a year, the cough that had debilitated D'Amato morphed into pneumonia. For two months he fought a ferocious losing battle, almost making it to the night of the championship that he had predicted awaited Mike Tyson. At one point, he ripped the IV out of his arm, demanding not to be sedated. Cus D'Amato died as he lived, believing to the end that mental toughness could win all battles.

Nine days after his death on November 13, 1985, Mike Tyson, with Kevin Rooney running the corner for the first time, knocked out a fighter billed as Fast Eddie Richardson in Houston, Texas. Fast forward to November 22, 1986. The time had come. The venue was the Las Vegas Hilton. The opponent was newly crowned WBC champion Trevor Berbick. The journey that began in the near-empty Catskill Boxing Club where Mike Tyson sparred with his first mentor, Bobby Stewart, while D'Amato and Atlas looked on, had come full circle.

D'Amato, who had told most of us back when he first introduced us to Tyson that here was the future champion, was about to become the all-time prophet in the world of boxing. His presence seemed to hover over the arena as Tyson, wearing a cutout towel transformed into a poncho in place of a robe, black boxing shoes, and no socks, looked history in the eye and won one for the old man of the Catskill Mountains.

Berbick had made it to his share of the finals by winning the WBC title with a classic jab, allied with a seventy-eight-inch reach. His plan was to keep Tyson at bay with that weapon and a seven-inch reach advantage. Almost immediately, Tyson solved his riddle by boring in underneath Berbick's jab with a barrage of ferocious right uppercuts. The ultimate finish was detonated with a five-punch, two-handed barrage. Berbick hit the floor so hard he made three attempts to rise but never got higher than his knees, falling backward each time.

The ring announcer proclaimed Tyson, at twenty years of age, the youngest heavyweight champion in history. Tyson did not climb the ring ropes to salute the crowd. With D'Amato so recently gone, there was no wild celebration.

"Mike used to visit Cus's grave once a week back then," explained Jay Bright, one of his Catskill housemates who had been in the corner that night. "When we got back to Catskill a day or so later, we took two glasses with us and went down to buy a bottle of champagne to take to Cus. Mike bought Moët, which was the most expensive one in the store. Cus used to preach to us about not wasting money, saying some day we would need that money. I told that to Mike, but he insisted we still get the high-priced champagne because it was for Cus.

"We went out to the Catskill cemetery and said a prayer. Then we made a toast and poured the rest on the grave. You could see the toll Cus's death had taken on Mike."

Four months later, Tyson had won all three major titles. He had been matched with James "Bonecrusher" Smith, who held two of them. Smith was taller and heavier, and very much a reluctant warrior. He clutched and grabbed and held. By the finish, a frustrated but triumphant Tyson had won every round.

Mike Tyson was a throwback to a time when the heavyweight champion would knock you out. The only way to beat him was to reverse that process, but nobody came close. America's sports fans yearn for the ultimate in thrills, a chain of explosive tableaus: the grand slam home run, the sixty-yard Hail Mary touchdown pass, the slam dunk that rattles the rim, and the most definitive punctuation mark to any athletic contest—the knockout. What made Tyson the poster boy for such moments was the fact that his early years shaped him with enough rage to complement the boxing skills D'Amato had given him. With this, Tyson returned the heavyweight division to the golden years of Joe Louis and Rocky Marciano. He was a ferocious puncher inside the ring and, more and more, a ferocious party guy outside of it.

Negotiations for a Spinks–Tyson fight were a testimony to the concept that less can morph into more. When Butch Lewis pulled Spinks out of the HBO tournament, HBO took Spinks to court. But Spinks had resigned his IBF title and a court ruled that, as a non-champion, he could not be held to his role in the competition that was contractually based on his owning a title.

Lewis's move was the trigger that made Spinks the solvent. By walking away from a moderately good paying gig, Spinks's purse to fight Tyson subsequently escalated to an incredible $13.5 million. Once set in motion, Tyson added fuel to the fire when he told Abraham, who owned the pay-per-view rights, "I want this fight. It's unfinished business. So, make the fight." Spinks–Tyson was scheduled for June 27, 1988, just three months after Jimmy Jacobs died of leukemia.

Against that background, with the mega fight in the talking stages, Tyson met and married a TV actress named Robin Givens, known for her role in the sitcom, *Head of the Class.* The marriage, almost from the start, rocketed toward an explosive end a year later. Her mother, Ruth Roper, was no stranger to negative press, and together their alliance resulted in a recipe for disaster for Tyson. Cutting through the barrage of all the innuendo, half-truths, planted newspaper rumors, and even Donald Trump's interference in contract negotiations between Tyson and Cayton, a single encounter that I had with the champion remains a haunting memory in the backroads of my mind.

I had scheduled a one-on-one interview with Tyson after his last pre-fight workout at the Trump Plaza Hotel in Atlantic City where he was headquartered. It was the Wednesday of fight week, and I was sitting with Chris Thorne, the boxing writer for my paper, *The Star-Ledger*, and Bill Gildea of *The Washington Post*. When the session was over, I headed for the dressing room upstairs and invited both of them to join me. I had no idea something so bizarre would happen that, without their presence, I would have hesitated to write it for fear of being disbelieved.

Tyson was cordial and cooperative. We talked about his typical mornings and how he did his running on the boardwalk early in the day. I asked if he previewed the fight in his mind as he ran. "No, no," he said. "I just sometimes think about things Cus told me." We both then laughed about the strange tone, and sometimes even stranger rhetoric, D'Amato used to employ, when suddenly his smile died abruptly, and he looked me directly in the eyes with a whole new expression clouding his face, which an instant ago had appeared so upbeat.

"I . . . I . . . just . . . why did Cus die . . . why did Jimmy [Jacobs] die on me? It used to be fun. Now it's only about the money . . . the money. Now there's nobody to trust or talk to."

Tyson was newly married, and his trainer, Kevin Rooney, was at his side. A just married man should be able to trust his wife regarding anything, and a fighter and his trainer are supposed to be able to discuss anything. But here he was, suddenly so alone. He leaned forward, dropped his head on my chest, and cried and cried and cried.

I had never seen anything like it. He certainly didn't know me that well. Our only common denominator was our relationship with D'Amato. His arms were around me as he cried, and I put mine around him. All my children were older than him. Then he pulled his head back and finished the interview, almost as though nothing had happened. My shirt was soaked. I had to go back upstairs to my room to change it.

Three hours later, I sat at the computer, still wondering as I typed out this sentence: "Atlantic City—The heavyweight champion of the world cried yesterday." Decades later, I still cannot explain what that moment meant, except to say that the contradictions I would see over and over in Mike Tyson in the years to come continually reminded me of a mystery in search of a Rosetta Stone.

But there would be no mystery three nights later at Convention Hall. Tyson had come into the arena angered by the barbs Spinks's manager, Butch Lewis, had publicly thrown at him. Additionally, he was frustrated by the fact that Spinks departing from the HBO tournament had left a major question mark hanging over Tyson's acceptance.

The final spur came when Lewis learned that Tyson's hands had been wrapped without anyone from the Spinks camp present. He charged into Tyson's dressing room and shouted at the commission representative, "Rewrap his hands now in front of us, or there will be no fight."

Years later, Lewis said of that moment, "I saw a chance to get into Mike's head, and I took it." Tyson began to punch the wall in a rage. On the other side of the wall, Spinks could hear his blows. Lewis sent for Eddie Futch, Spinks's trainer, and had Futch examine the way Tyson had been gloved. With Futch's approval, they returned to Spinks's dressing room.

Outside in the arena, the huge crowd was growing restless. It was a tick or two away from the time the fighters should have been in the ring. Finally, Spinks appeared, seemingly lost in thought. Afterward, he confessed, "I'm a fighter. It's what I do. I tried to take a shot but I came up short. Fear was knocking at my door big time."

In all probability, Spinks was not the only one to ever feel that type of intimidation while Tyson was at the other side of the ring. More realistically, it didn't matter. Spinks's attempts to stop the whirlwind was like leaning on a slender reed for support in a hurricane.

Tyson caught him with a left hook just ten seconds after the bell for round one. Spinks tried to clinch, but Tyson shoved him away. Referee Frank Cappuccino warned him, saying, "No more of that," but Tyson was already out of ear shot, moving forward and landing a left uppercut and right hand to the body. It was as though the air had gone out of Spinks, who dropped to a knee. He was up at four, but his legs were still unsteady. He threw a right hand wide, and Tyson hit him cleanly with a left and then a right to the head.

What was then the richest prize fight in history was over in just ninety-one seconds.

Tyson went on to stop Frank Bruno and Carl Williams. However, those closest to him sensed that something was wrong. The head movement and boxing skills that were the legacy of his time with D'Amato were not the same. Ignoring the basic boxing principles of loading up, he went for the one big knockout shot instead of setting up his opponent, getting away with it only because of the inferior qualities of his two opponents.

In truth, he seemed rudderless without D'Amato and Jacobs. Just before the Spinks fight, Robin Givens and her mother had badgered him into a renegotiation of his contract with Cayton, cutting out the only remaining member of the original trio's percentage of earnings. They induced Donald Trump to become their unpaid, unofficial advisor. That wasn't surprising considering that, according to Cayton, Trump had earlier tried to buy Tyson's contract from Cayton and was rebuffed with the words, "I don't need your money. I have my own. The contract is not for sale."

It had not taken long for the whirlwind romance between Tyson and Givens to turn into ashes. Givens and her mother were in the offices of Tyson's bank, demanding money. During a nationally televised interview with Barbara Walters, he sat motionless, head down, while Givens spoke of domestic abuse and physical intimidation and said she had become increasingly fearful of him. Emotionally and mentally, Tyson was in a state of disarray. The stage was set for a lucrative divorce.

Tyson's actions immediately compounded the situation. He broke a hand during a late-night Harlem street fight with boxer Mitch Green, then crashed his BMW into a tree while Givens was away watching the US Open tennis championships. *The Daily News* reported that it was a suicide attempt and that Tyson had an official diagnosis of bipolar disorder. Ultimately, Givens filed for divorce, and Tyson countersued. In the middle of all this, Tyson announced that Don King would be his exclusive promoter, with Cayton continuing as manager at a reduced percentage. King had long sought to handle Tyson. When the feud erupted with Givens and Roper on the one hand and Cayton on the other, King knew he could be the ultimate winner by inserting himself into the battle. Now he had to choose sides. But how?

Marty Cohen, a well-known boxing figure, had been an amateur fighter, a promoter, a manager, and now at age ninety, a trusted advisor to King. "You've been around a long time," King said, when he sought Cohen's advice. "I can get this kid [Tyson], I'm sure, but first I have to decide: Do I go with the women, or Trump [who wanted to manage Tyson], or even Cayton? I have to find the best way in."

Cohen pushed his cowboy hat back on his head. "Don, do you know what the strongest material in the world is?" When King didn't respond, he continued, "I'll tell you. It's a single hair from a woman's genitals. It could pull a battleship. It started the Trojan War. Go with the women. That's the way in."

King did. And when the inevitable break-up between them and Tyson took shape, he was there to pick up the pieces after a furious discussion with the women involving a transfer of money that King claimed was illegal. "She wrote herself a check for a million dollars," King told me, "and when it came back she put some bullshit reason on the memo. But you can't alter the memo on a check that has been cashed. That's a crime." Robin Givens meekly accepted a trip to the Dominican Republic for a divorce.

Meanwhile, Tyson continued to win in the ring. He was 37–0 when he signed to fly to Japan to meet the same Buster Douglas who had lost as a late substitute in the HBO tournament. On paper this appeared to be no fight at all. Jimmy Vaccaro, the respected veteran linemaker at South Point Casino, initially posted Douglas as a 27–1 underdog. The money came in so heavily on Tyson despite the long odds that, in order to balance his books, Vaccaro had to lure the long shot betters in with even longer odds. Douglas closed as a record 42–1 underdog.

Tyson arrived in Tokyo and paid little attention to training. Was it overconfidence or his personal troubles? The answer was probably both. Steve Lott, his friend and an employee of Cayton, stayed in the same hotel as Tyson. A week or so before the fight, he was watching television with his door open when Tyson came in unannounced and sat next to Lott on the couch.

"He said nothing at first," Lott recalled, "just shook his head back and forth. Then he finally said, 'Robin just called and told me she and Ruth have been to the bank and put down a down payment on a house in New Jersey for us. She said it cost $4.1 million. I never should have married her. It was a terrible mistake. I never should have married her.'" According to Lott, he then put his head on Lott's shoulder and cried.

If that had been public knowledge, the odds against Douglas would have probably been cut in half.

The irony in what followed was that Cus D'Amato had once been asked by a reporter to draw up a hypothetical battle plan to defeat Tyson. It involved out-jabbing him, getting inside with power, getting out very quickly, and giving him nothing but an acute angle with which to attempt to land a hit. Although Douglas had never heard of this, D'Amato's theoretical plan matched exactly the strategy he used on the night of what some say was the greatest heavyweight title fight upset in history.

Tyson came roaring out of his corner at the bell, determined to knock out Douglas with a single lunging left hook. He threw a lot of them and missed many. The head movement that had made Tyson so elusive in the past was gone. His attack was wooden. He looked like a man trying to cross a mud puddle while wearing snow shoes.

Douglas's response was the perfect antidote to Tyson's desperation. It was to stick and move, stick and move—get in and quickly retreat. Tyson's only answer was to load up and throw off-balance punches. By the fifth round, his left eye was sealed shut. But power is still power. In the eighth, Tyson reached down and dropped Douglas with a right uppercut that nearly ended it.

At the very beginning of round nine, Tyson launched an assault calculated to finish his opponent. Suddenly, with a single uppercut, Douglas turned the fight around, causing Tyson to wobble back into the ropes. Douglas hammered him over and over. He survived, though barely. A round later, Douglas dropped Tyson with a four-punch combination. The fight was over.

And so, too, were the good times, the almost mythic reputation, and the happy endings. What was now on Tyson's immediate calendar was a total collapse—the key ingredients would first be incarceration, followed by total humiliation.

What had begun as the story of the boxing sorcerer's apprentice would now morph into an American tragedy.

THIRTEEN

The Bite Felt 'Round the World

> "If you don't learn to control [fear], it'll
> destroy you and everything around."
>
> —*Mike Tyson*

The career that looked as though it would outlast every other heavyweight on the planet was now in full free fall. It was more than the way Buster Douglas had stopped Mike Tyson, leaving in its wake a lasting image of Tyson sprawled on the canvas, desperately groping to reinsert his mouthpiece. It was more than his sullen refusal to do his roadwork and gym work in the telltale weeks before Douglas. It was more than the impact of his nightmare marriage to Robin Givens.

What it was, was all of the above in equal parts.

Additionally, there was the battle for the control of the mind and trust of Mike Tyson, an ongoing treadmill in which people rose and fell and rose again, like a flavor of the month.

Shelly Finkel was a latecomer to boxing. He had been a highly successful rock and roll promoter with acts like Vanilla Fudge and Mountain. His entrance into boxing was focused on something called Tomorrow's Champions, a partnership with boxing trainer and manager Lou Duva.

"Knowing Shelly and Tyson," says writer and historian Ron Borges, "I'm reasonably sure [Shelly's] pitch went something like, 'Listen, we're both New Yorkers. We understand each other. I don't need your money. I want to help you, and I can.'"

Initially, Jacobs and Cayton hadn't wanted the Spinks fight, which would take place later on June 27, 1988. During early negotiations, they felt there wasn't enough money. With all the chaos in the Tyson camp, even as King strengthened his role as Tyson's promoter, Finkel had become a kind of advisor. By that time, he had already managed a few champions. Finkel advised Tyson to fight Spinks, and Tyson and the women, who wanted an immediate payday, agreed.

Meanwhile, Finkel paid a visit to Cayton in his office. According to Steve Lott, a member of the Tyson camp, Finkel told Cayton that Jimmy Jacobs, before his death, had already promised him the closed circuit operations on the fight. Cayton asked Lorraine Jacobs, Jacobs's widow who happened to be in Cayton's office at the time, if she knew anything about such a promise, and she vigorously shook her head to indicate a no.

Nevertheless, Cayton turned the closed circuit operation for Tyson–Spinks over to Finkel.

The day before the fight, Tyson called Cayton for a favor. Rory Holloway, Tyson's old buddy and Catskill running mate, wanted to set up a sanctioned Tyson t-shirt operation, and he needed Cayton to walk them through the process.

Cayton spent the entire afternoon explaining the legalities, expenses, and merchandising procedures involved. They thanked him, and Tyson told Cayton he could name whatever percentage he wanted. Cayton declined, saying he had done it as a favor. Ironically, six years later—long after King, Robin Givens, and her mother had cut Cayton's managerial share to a third, and during yet another Tyson incarceration—Holloway and his friend, John Horne, who were both on Don King's payroll, officially became Tyson's co-managers of record. Before this mess could sink to the level of a country cesspool, King already had contracts that not only made him Tyson's promoter but also gave him 30 percent of his earnings, which was technically against the law.

The difference between King and Finkel is best expressed by Borges in a way that sums up a lot of the whirlpool that perennially swirled around Tyson. "You look at their two backgrounds, and the best way to explain it is the fact that Don King had no choice to be anything but what Don King was. But Shelly Finkel didn't have to be what Shelly Finkel became."

The fighter was in the middle of a circus once again, but he wasn't the ringmaster. Four months after the Buster Douglas disaster, Tyson was back in the ring against Henry Tillman, the man who had beat him out of an Olympic berth but who was now no match for what Tyson had become. Tyson handled him easily. Next, he stopped Alex Stewart and hard-punching Razor Ruddock. Three months later, he beat Ruddock again—but he had to go the distance. And then it all came to a crashing stop, not with a whimper but with the biggest single bang in Mike Tyson's life.

In July of 1991, The Reverend Charles Williams invited Tyson to participate as a guest celebrity in a beauty contest in Indianapolis. At a rehearsal, Tyson was attracted to a teenager from Rhode Island named Desiree Washington. He flirted with her and obtained her telephone number. That night at 1:36 a.m., he called her from his limo, and she agreed to get dressed and meet him downstairs. Up to that point, both Tyson's and Washington's stories were the same.

He later claimed that, once in the limo, he kissed and fondled her with no objection in return. She said that she was struggling to push him away. When they arrived at the Canterbury Hotel, according to Tyson, he went upstairs to check on his bodyguard. She followed, though she didn't explain the reasons why, in light of her story about the tussle in the limo. Tyson claimed they had sex with mutual consent. She said he raped her.

The trial was, as expected, a circus. For reasons nobody could explain, King brought in a Washington tax lawyer, Vince Fuller, to defend Tyson. Fuller had no experience in sex crime cases. The State of Indiana countered with a home-grown, street-smart special prosecutor named Greg Garrison. The difference in their experience was apparent after the trial when Garrison commented, "He was a fine lawyer, but he was in the wrong forum. They act more like they're standing behind a podium, where he's from. They don't do much sitting on the edge of the desk."

It was a polite way of saying that Fuller had been out-lawyered, which he was. Tyson was convicted and sentenced to ten years, four of which were suspended.

The appeal centered around the difference in lawyers. It was handled by lawyer Alan Dershowitz, who argued that Tyson had had faulty representation and who pressed the point that the trial judge had excluded three Tyson witnesses, including Washington's former boyfriend, Wayne Walker, with whom she had had consensual sex but whom she had accused of rape in order to placate her father. Walker had signed an affidavit to that effect.

Tyson spent three years in prison. Though not a model prisoner, he did not lack visitors. They came with hope in their hearts and honeyed promises dripping from their lips.

The unofficial "Anything Don King Can Do I Can Do Better" sweepstakes was on. Major leaguers and minor leaguers alike participated. The line formed on the left. Honest Shelly "He Never Stole a Boxcar" Finkel led the way, not discouraged by the two unanswered letters he had sent Tyson. Butch Lewis visited Tyson twenty times. Rock Newman came arm-in-arm with his fighter, Riddick Bowe. Among the minors, in person or through surrogates, were Murad

Muhammad and Akbar Muhammad. From afar, Don King quietly put a hundred thousand dollars in Tyson's prison commissary account and spoke with him by telephone almost every night.

Lewis was in the game but far from blinded by the light. He cast himself in the role of prophet by predicting that the lure of Tyson's and King's past relationship would put King back in the driver's seat. King was uncharacteristically reticent. What he strangely lacked in bombast he made up through action. The night before Tyson's release, he was finalizing plans to pick up Tyson in a limo.

There was a reason for his confidence. For a long time, Rory Holloway and John Horne, the shoe salesman whose brother knew Tyson, had been on King's payroll at six thousand dollars per week. Their principal assignment was to visit Tyson in prison every week.

On August 16, 1994, with no public fanfare, Tyson signed a contract in a prison visiting room making Horne and Holloway his official managers and giving King exclusive rights to promote Tyson through 1999. Seven months went by. Finkel had no idea. Neither did Lewis, nor did Newman. It would seem that Tyson had been signed, sealed, and was about to be delivered to King.

There was, however, a potential snag that would have given King at least one sleepless night. It began with a simple ceremony, the voluntary giving of one's life to God without reservation through Islam. The profession of faith is called *shahada*, and it can be professed from the ornate sites of worship in Saudi Arabia or in a storefront mosque in the heart of urban America. It is the public reaffirmation by every Muslim child (male or female) at puberty and of every convert at the precise moment in which he or she adopts a new religion.

In the prison chapel at the Indiana Youth Center, before a congregation comprised primarily of prison inmates, Mike Tyson took that step. "I bear witness that there is only one God, Allah. I bear witness that Muhammad is the messenger of Allah." When Tyson said those words, what had seemed to be a chiseled-in-stone road map of his professional future shattered into a million pieces. In terms of comeback, management, and future associations, nothing was as it once seemed so sure to be. King worried about the obvious. Was that ceremony a statement of independence, or would it be business as usual, with Don calling every shot?

The day Mike Tyson was to be released, an argument ensued that lasted two days. There are two stories as to what caused the confrontation.

The first was that Holloway had allegedly showed Tyson a check King had made out to Holloway with enough zeros to complete the area code for Saturn. The inference Tyson may have drawn was that Holloway had been paid to deliver him non-stop on a chartered plane to King, although Tyson had already planned to stop at the Islamic Society of North America to join a number of Muslims in a prayer led by his spiritual advisor and a volunteer at the youth center, Muhammad Siddeeq.

King was most anxious for Tyson not to stop at the mosque or anywhere else but instead head back to Ohio, where Tyson and King lived fewer than twenty miles apart. "King doesn't want Mike to be seen praying as a Muslim by the rest of the world on Saturday," charged Akbar Muhammad, a fight promoter. "If he starts this way and proves strong in the faith, then where can King go? What hold over Mike can he have? Can he tempt him with women or any of the other vices? And now that Tyson has begun his new life, can King get him to return to Sodom and Gomorrah? He doesn't want Mike to stop and sort it out." Traditionally, isolating a fighter and bringing him to a one-on-one with his promoter has always resulted in the promoter getting what he wants.

The second and more plausible reason had its genesis in a newspaper picture of King and HBO's Seth Abraham, along with an article that spoke of King already negotiating on Tyson's behalf. Without his permission.

In the first instance, a boxing source, who also happened to be a Muslim, told me the fighter allegedly screamed at King, "How dare you try to stop me from praying to my God?" In the second, far more credible, story, he is said to have shouted, "Who are you to negotiate for me without my permission when all these people have been coming here offering me deals?" Proponents of both explanations, however, agree on one thing. Mike Tyson cursed and ranted, putting into King a fear of a future without potentially the biggest money maker in the history of the sport.

Ultimately, the truth is that while Tyson's decision to pray at the mosque played out a worrying scene for King, it was never going to amount to anything. Tyson was safely with Holloway and Horne for forty-eight hours after his release. After all that noise and speculation, King was back in control. On the battlefield of boxing, victory often goes to the man with the tenacity of a pit bull, the patience of an inchworm, and the track record of Caligula. And in that time and place, Don King was the unchallenged wearer of the only triple crown.

In the spirit of the Grand Ole Opry, Mike Tyson was back after four years in prison and still looking for love in all the wrong places—in and out of the ring. He had returned to the role of Lucifer's apprentice. For his return to the fold, King produced the perfect sacrificial lamb for his first fight on August 19, 1995. Peter McNeeley's father, Tom, had once fought (or attempted to fight) Floyd Patterson as a tune-up for Patterson's night of reckoning against Sonny Liston. The minimal talents of the father were the son's basic boxing inheritance.

Peter McNeeley had been a marine. Before the moment of truth in the ring, McNeeley was elevated by King's rhetoric to a status equal to one of the men who had planted the American flag on Iwo Jima. Tyson destroyed him in eighty-nine seconds.

Next came Buster Mathis, Jr., representing a landmark case in the annals of New Jersey hypocrisy. The fight was rejected by New Jersey and shipped across the border to Philadelphia, marking, perhaps, the first time New Jersey successfully shipped its garbage somewhere else. The fight ended abruptly in the third round.

Now came the quest for titles. First up was Frank Bruno, the WBC champion, who did not survive the third round. Then came Bruce Seldon, who held the WBA title. Dropped at the start with a left hook and a right, and then a left and another right, Seldon lasted 109 seconds.

As Don King lit his post-fight cigar and Tyson appeared almost bored, it seemed that everything old was new again. But looming on the horizon was a test far greater than anyone could imagine. His name was Evander Holyfield.

The first time I saw Holyfield, he was an amateur light heavyweight at the 1984 Los Angeles Olympics. A few months earlier, he had been a teammate of Tyson's, training for the Olympics in Colorado Springs. Tyson didn't make it; Holyfield did.

Holyfield reached the semifinals, knocking out (a rarity in Olympic boxing) three fighters in a total of fewer than six rounds. He then faced Kevin Barry, a very willing but less skilled fighter from New Zealand. If he could deal with Barry as expected, he would face a Yugoslavian, Anton Josipović, in the final.

Holyfield was dominant on his way to the title round, hitting Barry often and hard. It was clear what was going to happen next.

Or so everyone thought. It would be neither man who would decide the match. The referee, Gligorije Novičić, was also a Yugoslavian. He had already violated the rules by giving Barry enough warnings for disqualification, but he continued to ignore the obvious. With just six seconds left in round two, Holyfield landed a right to the body, followed by a classic boxing punctuation mark, a left hook to the head. Barry fell like a stone. Novičić proceeded to screw up the entire situation (perhaps intentionally). First he counted Barry out, as he should have. Then he disqualified Holyfield for "hitting when

I said break." For the record, he had said it between punches, when Barry was already falling and Holyfield, as every fighter is taught to do, had just added the finishing touch to his combination.

Holyfield had been shafted, and Barry was in no condition to fight the final. The Yugoslavian light heavyweight won against his shadow. However, in that instant, Evander Holyfield became an American hero.

In the years that followed, America watched him win the light heavyweight title and the cruiserweight title, as well as earn a match against Buster Douglas, the long-shot title holder who had defeated Tyson. It was clear that Douglas had no chance against Holyfield even before the opening bell. When he shed his bathrobe to step on the scale for the traditional weigh-in, we were not looking at Buster the miracle maker, but instead at Buster the beached whale. He had ballooned to 246 pounds, fifteen above his fighting weight. In the third round, Douglas, already laboring, tried to throw an uppercut, missed, and took a straight right than knocked him down and ended it.

Holyfield won all of Douglas's titles and defended the one he already had. But it did not take long for the magnetism to peel off the Cinderella story. He successfully defended them in two dramatic fights against George Foreman and Bert Cooper and decisioned Larry Holmes. Then he lost his titles almost immediately to Riddick Bowe in a savage twelve-round fight. He won them back in the rematch a year later and immediately lost them again to Michael Moorer.

In the blink of an eye, Holyfield's résumé had gone from a trail of magnificent fairy dust to the residue of yesterday's talcum powder. He had become a former hero treading water. In short, the reselling of Evander Holyfield to America had fallen into the category of a typical Don King sales pitch: "Only in America . . . a country of second chances . . . hadn't King himself and Mike Tyson, King's tiger, gotten those chances, too . . . hand me that flag, brother, I know how to wave it. . . ."

King sold his Tyson–Holyfield fight as only he could, but the pay-per-view public was not so quick to buy. When Vegas posted its first line on the fight, Holyfield was a 25–1 underdog. By fight week, it had slimmed down to a legitimate 12–1. Two days before the actual fight, three bets of ten thousand dollars or more were placed on Holyfield. By fight time, those odds had fallen to 7–1.

Holyfield arrived in town on Monday and immediately proclaimed, "God will enable me to do anything I want to do in this fight." It did not impress most of the regulars in Sodom and Gomorrah in the desert. History pretty much seemed to support the theory that once the house set the line and adjusted it, divine intervention is generally marked absent.

Ever since his amateur days, the aura of intimidation had always been a silent weapon in Mike Tyson's arsenal. The night before Holyfield–Tyson, November 9, 1996, it was alive and angry in Holyfield's hotel room.

The memory is still vivid in his mind. Years afterward he would tell Tom Hauser, the erudite boxing columnist, reporter, and historian, "I must have got out of bed a hundred times that night. I shadow boxed. I read the Bible. I went back to bed. I couldn't sleep. I read the Bible again. Then I shadow boxed again. I had no more than three hours of sleep.

"When I finally got into the ring, my legs felt weak. They felt like they were made of Jello. Then the bell rang. My legs came back. I did my job."

But at the very start, he almost did not.

Tyson approached him, feinted with his left shoulder, and came back with a stunning right cross. It would be Tyson's best punch of the fight, and it certainly got Holyfield's attention. But then Holyfield did something that immediately put his personal signature all over the evening: He tied Tyson up and walked him back toward the ropes. Both fighters and both corners knew exactly what that meant. By putting Tyson where he didn't want to go, Holyfield had immediately established that he was the stronger of the two, winning him the geography of the ring. Frustrated, Tyson hit him after the bell, with bad intentions. Holyfield clocked him right back.

It was an instructive first round. By punching, landing, holding, and pushing Tyson around, the pattern for a stunning upset was set. Styles make fights, and Holyfield's offered yet another problem. As he moved in and they clinched, several head butts were ruled accidental by the referee, Mitch Halpern, but claimed intentional by Tyson.

In the third round, Holyfield began to land combinations. He ripped the body with an uppercut midway through the round and followed with a right cross down the middle. It was a pattern that became repetitive. Tyson had no answer for it. He was dazed and confused, admitting after the fight, "By the third round I didn't know where I was."

In the fifth, Tyson rallied and had what may have been his best round; however, a round later, the disbelief of the crowd morphed into a vociferous chant of "Holyfield . . . Holyfield . . . Holyfield" after Evander drove him back with a well-placed left hook that first staggered and then dropped hm. For the second time in his entire professional career, Mike Tyson had to get up off the deck. It all led up to the tenth round, probably the worst beating Tyson ever took. Midway through the round, Holyfield unleashed a one-two combination. He seemed to brush off a right by Tyson that had landed on his jaw with no impact. Then Holyfield was all over the weary Tyson with a right-left-right assault, followed by too many punches to count. Miraculously, Tyson would not go down. He staggered back. He bounced against the ropes. He reeled forward. His moves were a blend of kamikaze pilot and Spartan warrior—and history tells us how both of them always finished: bravely beaten.

Tyson answered the bell for round eleven, caught two lefts and three rights, and Halpern stepped in to end it after just thirty-seven seconds.

Of course, there would be a rematch. But would it sell?

It was not exactly a secret how badly Tyson had lost. The truth was that Evander Holyfield beat him like a bass drum. The question now in the minds, hearts, and cash registers of the Don King Marching and Chowder Society was, *Where has Michael gone?*

Part of him had been gone ever since Kevin Rooney, his original pro trainer, was fired before the Spinks fight at Don King's insistence. Gone along with him was the head movement that had been Tyson's hole card. Gone were the power punches he once threw in bunches. And gone, most noticeably, was the intimidation factor with which he had ruled out the best heavyweights in the world.

And Evander Holyfield had capitalized on each retrogression. Now, Tyson would be coming to the rematch with Richie Giachetti, an old King standby, as trainer and Rory Holloway and John Horne as unproven front men. There was a desperate awareness that this rematch, set on June 28, 1997, would be a fork-in-the-road point that great fighters must always face.

Trouble surfaced at a pre-fight rules meeting. King, Horne, and Holloway all spoke in favor of removing Mitch Halpern, the referee in the first fight, who had been scheduled to work the rematch. The Holyfield camp argued that Halpern was fine with them and should stay. The Tyson camp persisted in their objections. Finally, Horne threatened that there could be a possibility of no fight, telling the commission, "All I'm saying is that you consider Mike Tyson. If it weren't for him, you wouldn't be sitting there. I'm only in this state because of him. When he leaves, I'm gone." Faced with such an ineffectual threat, the commission voted that Halpern stay.

However, boxing is boxing. Someone above the commission spoke with King and made a call. The only person who was above the commission was the governor. Mills Lane, a former Washoe County district attorney and now a judge from Reno, who was also one of the best referees in the world, replaced Halpern. Ironically this new referee chosen by the Tyson camp would later be the one who would disqualify him.

From the beginning of the bout, the MGM Grand Garden Arena was electric. Doubts about Tyson, who was still a slight favorite by the local sports books to win, coupled with a new respect for Holyfield, split the crowd into two partisan camps. King had named the fight "The Sound and the Fury," and surely the crowd provided that sound right from the start. The fury would surface later, and nobody on the planet could ever claim to have expected the way in which it manifested itself.

Tyson fought better, with more head movement and more punches with bad intentions. The first round appeared to be even slower paced than in their first fight. Then, a straight overhand right punch staggered Tyson, winning what had been a close round, though Tyson managed to push Holyfield backward. It seemed as though we were to have a real fight in the making.

In round two, as Holyfield began to pile up his advantage, Tyson threw a ferocious right hand. Holyfield, the taller of the two, ducked underneath, and their heads bumped. Blood poured from around Tyson's right eye.

Butting had been Tyson's complaint in the first fight. Now, he and Giachetti screamed their complaints at Lane, who reviewed the tape between rounds and ruled it an "unintentional head butt." At the start of round three, Lane threw up his hands and sent Tyson back to his corner. He had apparently spit out his mouthpiece just before the bell—a clue to Tyson's state of mind and his intentions—and the sign of the end of all the rules in this fight.

Holyfield nailed Tyson with a one-two that rocked him. But Tyson had already made his choice. When Holyfield came inside and ducked his head, Tyson grabbed his shoulder, put him in a headlock, and sank his teeth in his right ear with all the restraint of an angry pit bull. Holyfield jumped as though he had been hit by an electric shock. Lane examined the bite and deducted two points.

"You bit him in the ear," Lane said to Tyson.

"That was a punch," said Tyson.

"Bullshit," said Lane. "One more, and you're out of here."

Whatever punches were thrown afterward came from Holyfield. At one point, it appeared as though Tyson had slammed his arm into Holyfield's arm, intending to break it. At the bell, both of Holyfield's ears were leaking blood. Lane went to the corner and examined what he now saw as two different bites. Lane ended the fight.

Security immediately surrounded Holyfield and his trainer, Tommy Brooks. Tyson repeatedly tried to rush across the ring to get at him. Fights broke out in and out of the ring. It took twenty-five minutes to restore order.

Up in the main hotel, after the crowd began to rush out of the arena, a sound echoed from upstairs, a *pop . . . pop . . . pop*. It was followed by a human stampede when somebody hollered that shots were being fired. People threw themselves on the floor up and down the hallway that led to the casino. Dave Anderson, the talented Pulitzer Prize–winner from *The New York Times*, recalled that he took shelter behind a pillar near the food court. People dove under tables there and further down toward the restaurant area. Pat English, the lawyer for Main Events, the group that had represented Holyfield from the beginning, hit the floor just outside Wolfgang Puck's restaurant.

After I had finished writing my account of the fight from ringside and sent it to my paper, I walked up the arena's stairs and into the casino toward the hotel elevators. I did not see a single person. The place was stone-cold empty, and I suddenly realized I was hearing something I had never heard before or since in any casino or hotel anywhere—sheer, hollow, empty silence. The hotel, its casino, its lobby, and its restaurants were as silent as the sound of one hand applauding, for the first time since the great fire at the original MGM had totally evacuated the building in 1980.

The night ended not with a celebration but with a haunting. There was not a single human at a green felt table, not a person in front of a slot machine, not the familiar slap of cards hitting the tables, no music announcing a jackpot along the hundreds of rows of slot machine.

I am sure the casino lied the next day. They attributed the *pops* to the sound of champagne corks being removed, instead of gun fire. Well, what did you expect? Money runs the casinos and the casinos run the town, and that's just one of the lies that was told in Vegas—and that sure as hell will stay in Vegas.

FOURTEEN

Other Contenders and George's Curtain Call

"If bluebirds can fly across the rainbow, why can't I?"

—*George Foreman*

It was the end of the golden age of heavyweights—but not the end of Mike Tyson. Too many people had had their hands in the Tyson cookie jar, and so he fought on, first off bad advice and ego, and in the end just to pay the bills as the debts mounted.

But it was Tyson himself who put the punctuation mark to the end of that magnificent era. The disgraceful biting of Holyfield's ears diminished his fading reputation, and the heavyweights were never the same.

His time was past, and his last major stand was against Lennox Lewis in Memphis before a huge crowd disguised as empty seats. In the pre-fight press conference in New York, Tyson raced across the stage to physically attack Lewis. In the scramble that followed, he bit Lewis on the leg, then singled out a reporter whom he called a homosexual and said, and I'm paraphrasing, that he would rape him and make him like it, all the while rubbing his crotch throughout this hysterical monologue.

Tyson's charm remained consistent during his training, to the point where Tyson–Lewis was shaping up as a match between the champion, wearing a white hat, and the challenger, wearing a ski mask. The fight itself was totally lopsided. Lewis's trainer, Emanuel Steward, did not like the way referee Eddie Cotton was officiating, and pleaded with Lewis in the corner, "Listen, will you please knock this motherfucker out, please. If you don't, they will try to steal this from you. Do it."

By the seventh round, Tyson was helpless and hopeless. In the eighth, he was knocked down twice and counted out. He still had to pay bills, and he was broke. His last two fights, against journeymen, were a disaster. He left the business a shell of what he had once been. The comet had long since crashed and burned.

And what about Lennox? Was he good enough to be considered part of the golden heavyweight era as chronicled in this book? For starters, he had come along too late and had fought too few of those great contenders. Although a talented fighter, he doesn't make the cut. Nor does Riddick Bowe, a champion like Lewis who had three great fights with Holyfield, but who just didn't fight enough against the best to make it into our elite group.

There were many others who didn't make the list, although they were genuinely part of that golden era. Sadly, they would have been champions in the next generation but were born too soon. Here they are, in no particular order.

Earnie Shavers, the hardest one-punch hitter I ever saw, and perhaps the hardest one-punch heavyweight of the whole era. Incredibly, sixty-eight of his seventy-four wins were by knockout. He fought all the great ones who were brave enough to fight him, and not every one of them was. He hit Holmes so hard he fell face down but got up to win. Ali admitted to me, "I was unconscious on my feet in the fifteenth round, but I somehow won that round. Nobody ever hit me as hard as he did." Ali had never been booed as much as he was when it was revealed to the Madison Square Garden crowd that all three judges had scored that fight 9–6 in his favor.

Oscar Bonavena, who almost knocked Joe Frazier out of the ring. Bonavena lost that title fight against Frazier and a subsequent box-off to Ali, an elimination fight that Ali had to win in order to set up Ali–Frazier I. To win it, it took the best left hook Ali ever threw in his life to lock it up with a three-knockdown explosion in the final round.

Ali was the only one to knock him out in Bonavena's twelve-year career. Indeed, Bonavena was a contender with proven power, a wild-swinging, wild-living heavyweight out of Argentina. More bull than boxer, he had tremendous strength, could punch with both hands, and was fearless. Inside the ring, he tended to be awkward, but he was still a definite threat as long as he threw his jackhammer punches. However, outside the ring, his lifestyle cost him his own life, dooming him to failure after he met a man named Joe Conforte, who made a fortune with legal houses of prostitution.

Conforte, who was also involved in boxing, met Bonavena, then a top ten fighter, in the fighting circle. Conforte's wife, Sally, was the madam for the hookers at his Bunny Ranch. Conforte invited Bonavena to visit and train for a while at the ranch. Trouble came about when the fighter and the madam became an item. Although she knew nothing about boxing, Bonavena made her his manager. He and Confote clashed repeatedly. When Bonavena was told to leave, Sally left with him, and they were told never to come back. But they did—or tried to. Bonavena began telling people around town that he was about to take over the ranch's business. During their last confrontation, one of Conforte's bodyguards shot him dead.

Ron Lyle, who was put in Colorado state prison at age nineteen for eleven years for a gang murder charge. After surviving a stabbing that was nearly fatal, he learned to box. Lyle turned pro in 1964 and embarked on a career that spanned fifteen-plus years in which he won forty-three of fifty-one fights with his awesome punching power. But he could never nail the big ones, though he scared the hell out of both Ali and Foreman. In the fourth round against Foreman, Lyle came within two or three punches of his greatest win. He knocked Foreman down twice and had him holding on toward the end, but ultimately let him get away in the next round, when Foreman stopped him. Against Ali, Lyle was ahead on all three judges' cards. Ali knew he was in deep trouble. He caught Lyle in the corner with a barrage of eleven unanswered punches, and they stopped it. Power was Lyle's game, and in any other era he would have been a champion.

Jerry Quarry, who would, and did, fight everyone. Quarry was the fighter who agreed to be the opponent for Ali's comeback; however, a decisive cut above the eye cost him any chance in that fight. He performed well against all the dominant fighters of his era but never won a title. Although he didn't have the same power as some of those mentioned here, he boxed very well and his ring skills were respected by the best of his time.

Cleveland Williams, the greatly underrated fighter with the body of a sculptor's model (which he had been) and tremendous right hand power. Sonny Liston repeatedly said that Williams hit him harder than any other fighter in his career. Liston had reason to remember, especially after that one night in Miami when Williams nearly knocked Liston out of the ring. Sadly, by the time he got his chance against Ali, he was finished. A Texas cop had senselessly pumped three bullets into him over a ridiculous traffic stop on a deserted highway near Houston called Jackrabbit Road. The cop was mysteriously held blameless, and Williams fought Ali with a bullet still in his spleen. Under those circumstances, the knockout Ali administered was pre-ordained. "I died three times on that operating table," Williams said, on his decision to fight right after the incident. "If He didn't want me to fight, He'd have let me stay dead, because fighting's the only thing I know."

And finally, "Big George" Foreman. This postscript would be incomplete were it not to return to the amazing man who had held the title briefly but failed to remain a genuine factor during the golden age. Foreman lost it decisively to Ali and, after a few more fights, retired and became a minister.

I was in Puerto Rico when neither fighter had a title and Jimmy Young administered the worst beating George Foreman ever had. It was, we were led to believe, Foreman's last fight. He had to be helped down the ring steps by his handlers. In the dressing room, he either spoke in "tongues," as he still believes, or just babbled, overcome by heat prostration. It was clear, however, that his belief led him to retire in 1977.

I thought I would never see him fight again. Then, sometime around 1982, I saw a wire service photo of him in our newspaper in which he held a Bible in one hand and a bullhorn in the other. He was on the streets in Marshall, Texas, preaching the gospel. Five years later, he announced a comeback in which nobody, including me, believed. I called some fight people in Texas and left messages for him.

I received his call at 3 a.m. We talked a little about boxing and a lot about the Bible. After two more post-midnight phone calls, I told him I was tired of the auditions and said I was going to write about him the next day.

The strangest comeback in boxing history had begun. Incredibly, Foreman got a title shot against Holyfield in Atlantic City. Though he didn't win it, it was a brutal fight, one that raised newfound respect for his amazing return to the ring.

And he wasn't through yet. In 1994, at age forty-five, George Foreman signed to meet Michael Moorer, the IBF and WBA champion. Mindful of the drama, Foreman wore the same red trunks he had worn back in 1974 against Muhammad Ali. But this time, unlike that long-gone night in Zaire, Foreman's façade of invincibility had no believers. He was a major underdog. "Moorer called me a phony and a fake," Foreman said, "and I guess I am in all things except my religion. But I do sell cheeseburgers and hotdogs. I'm a salesman, and I get people into the tent. But after this fight you'll still know where to find me. I'll be preachin' in Houston on Wednesday night."

The first nine rounds proved the validity of Foreman's new underdog status. Moorer positively dissected Foreman's lumbering defense. Moorer moved easily, coming inside behind the jab and then boxing George's head off.

When they came out for the tenth round, Foreman's right eye was nearly swollen shut. He moved more with a shuffle than a stride. He lurched forward, desperately hoping to land one huge shot to end it. He needed an opening, and Moorer gave it to him.

Moorer moved inside. Foreman threw a jab, and Moorer walked straight into the trap. Instead of moving his head back at an angle, Moorer froze. Foreman threw his right hand, climbed his highest mountain, and planted his flag. Moorer lay on the canvas, his legs splayed in opposite directions. The fight was over.

That night, Foreman and I talked about Zaire and the burden it had placed on him for years. His victory against Moorer was more exorcism than knockout. Foreman's comeback was one for the ages, and so was his final quote: "If bluebirds can fly across the rainbow, why can't I? If you're forty or fifty and they tell you that you can't do something, think again. If you think you can, then you can."

Those who were there to witness it still swear it wasn't a bluebird at all. What it was, was a full-blown eagle. And the measured sound of the voice of the knockdown time keeper was drowned out by the flapping of its wings. I could swear I heard it, even if nobody else did.

It was the sound of a chorus of trumpets as the preacher man huffed and puffed and the metaphorical walls of Jericho came tumbling down on top of Michael Moorer's head.

It was a haunting, straight out of the archives of the time, when once there were giants.

EPILOGUE

> "Now you will not swell the rout
> Of lads that wore their honors out,
> Runners whom renown outran
> And the name died before the man."
>
> —*A Shropshire Lad, A. E. Housman*

They are gone now. Sonny Liston and Floyd Patterson; Muhammad Ali, Joe Frazier, and Ken Norton. They passed away with their legacies intact. George Foreman is preaching the Word and selling his grills. Larry Holmes never left Easton, Pennsylvania. Mike Tyson has morphed from Iron Mike into Mr. Tyson, actor and raconteur.

But in this cruel and beautiful sport, as a class they stand above every heavyweight group that preceded them or that would follow them. In the backroads of my mind, I still see them as they were— young and strong and proud, and in the return of George Foreman not so young but still strong and still proud.

The operative word for this whole amazing era was, indeed, *pride*. Pride was the spur on a broiling day in an arena without air-conditioning when Muhammad Ali and Joe Frazier fought the brutal fight Ali described as "the closest thing to death you will ever see." Neither would quit, though both had more than a little opportunity to do so.

Pride? Frazier told me how deeply Ali's name-calling had wounded him when his children came home from school crying because the other kids said Ali had called their father a gorilla.

211

Pride? Long after that trial by fire in Manila, Ali explained how and why it drove him. "Somebody fights me and loses, and it doesn't mean much except that they lost a prize fight. But if I lose, kids in Harlem cry." In Manila, both of them had fought for far more than a championship belt.

Pride? It was the amazing emotional glue that held this whole generation of heavyweights in its grasp and formed an unbreakable fraternal tie among them, which lasted long after they quit the ring. Consider these other examples.

The night Mike Tyson bit both Evander Holyfield's ears, anger and an intense frustration had boiled over in Tyson's psyche. On the other hand, pride was the unspoken catalyst that continued to fuel Holyfield. As the action was halted after the first bite, the referee, Mills Lane, walked toward Holyfield's corner and yelled, "If you can't continue, I'll forfeit the thing to you." According to Teddy Atlas, Don Turner, Holyfield's trainer, turned to him and said, "Take it. You get the title."

But Holyfield shocked ringsiders, speaking through broken lips as blood poured down from one ear: "Put the damned mouthpiece back in my mouth. I am going to fuckin' knock that son of a bitch out."

It was the same with Larry Holmes during a closed door training session at Caesars Palace, six days before Holmes would fight Ken Norton for the world heavyweight championship. The gym was silent except for the squeaky sound of boxing shoes against the floor. Holmes threw a hook to the body of his sparring partner, Luis Rodriguez, and even as it connected he knew he had torn a ligament in his left arm. When told by the doctor that he shouldn't fight, Holmes approached Keith Kleven, the local therapist, who worked on his arm every day. On fight night, Kleven stood in the corner with the warning, "If you get hit on that spot, there will be nothing more I can do for you."

Many years later, Holmes explained his thought process to me. "We had secret discussions about not going through with the fight if I had just one arm. But it was going to be my decision, and I knew I was going to fight even if they had to cut my arm off. It was the title, man. This is why we fight. This was a matter of pride on which you can't give up.

"On fight night, I piled up an early lead, and then about halfway through I got hit on the arm. I hardly used it after that until the last round. In those days, we fought fifteen. When the bell rang, I said, *fuck the pain*. This is the title. I won't be able to look myself in the mirror again if I don't use that arm and lose the fight.

"It was a dead-even fight going into the fifteenth. He nailed me early, and I was hurt. Then I nailed him with a left uppercut and he was wobbling at the end—and I won it. If you say it was pride that kept me going, you are probably right."

And finally, in the own words of Chuck Wepner: "I was always proud of what I did. Yeah, I bled a lot in my career. They nicknamed me the Bayonne Bleeder. But I went the whole route with Ali. I won fifty-seven fights. When I fought Sonny Liston, I needed seventy-two stitches, but I wouldn't quit.

"You ask me about pride? My last fight, I didn't have much left. I fought on pride alone. I was thirty-seven years old, and it was against Scott Frank who was younger and on his way up. Going into the last round, I thought, *what the hell am I doing here?* I'm hurt. I lost nine rounds. The ref asked me if I wanted to keep going, and I said, 'I will finish this fight with the last breath in my body if I have to. It's the only way I can go out.'"

It was an era in which this remarkable generation of heavyweights took their show on the road more than any other and lit up arenas and stadiums from Los Angeles to New York, from Reno and Las Vegas to Detroit and Minneapolis, with stops in between from England to Germany, Africa to Malaysia, and even to the Philippines.

Once, they were the crown jewels of all of boxing's weight classes. But stop somebody on the street today and ask who the heavyweight champion of the planet is, and he won't be able to tell you. That means there isn't any. Today, it's all about too many inept governing bodies, too many titles, and too few genuine heavyweight fighters. In this country, the biggest and the best of our two-hundred-pound athletes become power forwards or tight ends. Now, only the hungry fight like heavyweight champions should. That's why Eastern Europe is where most of them come from.

But this story isn't about them. It's about tunes of glory we used to hear and legends who brought a new dimension of pride and determination into the ring. What a generation, and what a ride, they gave us.

Somebody should build a monument to them.

Somebody did. His name was Muhammad Ali.

Long after the last fighters left, Ali's monument still stood halfway between Reading and Pottsville in Pennsylvania's lush Schuylkill County. Who better than Muhammad Ali to be its architect? To oversee the building of Ali's dream project, he enlisted the help of his long-time friend and personal business manager, Gene Kilroy.

Nestled in the woods around Deer Lake, Pennsylvania, it was known as Muhammad Ali's Deer Lake training camp. It was a cluster of log cabins that included a kitchen, a chapel, Ali's sleeping quarters, a gym, and several other cabins for sparring partners and Ali's guests. Just before the Foreman fight, I had brought my own kids to the camp with me while I filmed a television show. Ali shook hands with my son, then swooped down to pick up my little daughter and held her high over his head as she giggled.

"Is that your daddy? Don't lie to me. Is that your daddy? That's not your daddy. That man is ugly and you are beautiful. The Gypsies musta brung you. Gimme a kiss."

It was here in Deer Lake that hot paraffin baths healed Ali's arthritic hands. Watching him hit the heavy bag, I was convinced he would knock Foreman out—and I wrote about it. "Listen, Jerry," Ali said, "if you think the world was shocked when Nixon resigned, just wait until I kick Foreman's behind."

It was here that Ali chopped wood and moved boulders to build himself up. He built a lane he called Fighters Heaven, lined with eighteen boulders on which he personally painted the names of the greatest fighters who ever lived—Dempsey, Louis, Marciano—all except his own. I suspected he believed there was no boulder big enough for him.

It was here that the famed entourage lived together like frat boys: Gene Kilroy, the personal business manager, camp facilitator, keeper of the checkbook, and restorer of order; Pat Patterson, the Chicago-cop-turned-security-chief; Angelo Dundee, the venerable trainer; Drew Bundini Brown, the witch doctor and cheerleader; and Wali Muhammad, the bucket man and timekeeper.

There never was and never will be a group that belonged together as much as this one had. Most of them are gone now, but in my mind they remain eternally young.

A quarter of a century ago, I went back to the deserted camp at Deer Lake. I wandered into the old camp kitchen where the wall plaque with a list of kitchen rules hung thick with dust. The long wooden table and chairs were empty. I walked down the hill to the little gym that surely must remain a refuge to the ghosts and echoes of a younger Ali at work.

The thump of gloved fists against heavy bag and the rat-tat-tat of the speed bag. The sound of the three-minute-bell ringing and Wali Muhammad, a towel around his neck and a stopwatch in his hand, yelling, "Time!" A gritty shell of a hand wrap, discarded perhaps twenty-five years earlier, lay on the ring floor.

It was getting along toward sunset now, and as I stepped outside and walked back up the hill, the rickety sign was still there, swaying back and forth in the wind.

MUHAMMAD ALI TRAINING CAMP.

Beneath it, another wooden slat read:

NO TRAINING TODAY.

In that moment, the wind began to gust, and from somewhere deep in the backroads of my mind I could swear I heard a familiar voice whispering:

"I'm still the greatest."

Who says you can't go home again?

THE END

ACKNOWLEDGMENTS

I would like to acknowledge the patience and guidance of my friend and agent Peter Sawyer, the vision of Herman Graf, who saw what other publishers did not, the professionalism of my editor Kim Lim, Bob Izenberg who handled the heavy lifting with my stuttering computer, and my special friendships with Gene Kilroy and Muhammad Ali.

I also want to issue a special thanks to every fighter, manager, trainer, hustler, promoter, and mobster who appears in this book. Without them, there never would have been a golden age of heavyweight boxing.